The Lost Glory

Dave Markee

Sovereign World

Sovereign World Ltd
PO Box 777
Tonbridge
Kent TN11 0ZS
England

ISBN 1 85240 257 1

This Sovereign World book is distributed in North America by Renew Books, a ministry of Gospel Light, Ventura, California, USA. For a free catalog of resources from Renew Books/Gospel Light, please contact your Christian supplier or call 1-800-4-GOSPEL.

Typeset by CRB Associates, Reepham, Norfolk.
Printed in England by Clays Ltd, St Ives plc.

Contents

About the Author

As a professional bass player, Dave Markee has worked with many of the world's finest musicians. He has recorded and toured with such luminaries as The Who, Joan Armatrading, Leo Sayer, Alan Price, Bing Crosby, Ben Webster, Maynard Ferguson, Chris Rea, and many more. He worked with Henry Mancini on two *Pink Panther* films and became a member of the Eric Clapton band in 1979, touring and recording with him for $3\frac{1}{2}$ years. He is still in demand as a highly respected session bassist.

Dave is the senior pastor of Folly's End, a vibrant and growing church in South London, United Kingdom. Together with his wife, Ze, Dave teaches and leads worship internationally.

You can find out more about the work of Folly's End Church by visiting their web site at www.follysend.org

Acknowledgements

As with most revelation God gives us, some thoughts and principles shared in this book have been 'distilled' over time, while some are very recent. Issues that have been on my heart for a long time have grown in passion and urgency. My desire is to share them with you, and my prayer is that through them you will be truly released into the full potential of your God-given creativity.

I would like to thank Leo Soloman and Norman Beane who first encouraged me to play the bass and gave me such a great start at the Shell Bar Jazz Club, Cleethorpes, and in the Bob Walker Big Band. To Bryn and Sally Howarth, who loved me unconditionally and took our whole family to meet their friend Jesus. James Ryle, for the courageous revelation that first challenged me to think seriously about creativity. John and Paula Sandford, whose prophetic lives and writing have given the Body of Christ foundations of inestimable value in the area of biblical sanctification. John and Carol Arnott – your gleeful enjoyment of the Holy Spirit and His work has been nothing short of inspirational. John Menlove and Dan Cutrona, for practical help and spiritual encouragement in a very dark hour. Dr Myles Munroe of the Bahamas, for his warm friendship and teaching, especially on destiny and purpose. Dr Patricia Morgan of Oral Roberts University and Kingston, Jamaica, for her prophetic input into my personal life and that of Folly's End Christian Schools, Croydon. Melinda Fish, who encouraged me to write this book in the first place. Jeremy Sinott of TACF for his encouragement and Tim Pettingale, my new friend and editor. Here's to many more Tim!

Also to the many wonderful and gifted musicians I have had the privilege of working with and listening to over the years. It is with deep respect that I dedicate this book to you and pray that all of you would come to know the One who gave you such awesome gifts.

To my family, Sarah, Rick, Alison and Jessica, Daniel, Imogen and Jack; the leaders, staff and people of Folly's End Church, Croydon, and the best gift God ever me, my wonderful wife and partner, Ze.

Dave Markee
Folly's End, Croydon
September 1999

What Others Are Saying About *The Lost Glory*

If as a man thinks in his heart so is he, then whoever controls the thoughts of a man controls the man. The most powerful force on earth is the spoken word. Why? Because words are the containers of thought. However, the most effective force on earth is when that word is placed in the stream of music. The word 'music' is derived from the root word 'muse', which means 'to make think; or control thought'. Therefore the goal of music is to control and condition the thought life of another. You would recall the role of David and his music in the life of King Saul. It is also interesting to note that the largest book in the inspired content of scripture is a songbook – Psalms.

However, the most striking thought is to remember that Lucifer, the fallen angel, was the chief musician and worship leader in heaven. Thus we should understand why his desire is still to control this area of God's creation, because it controls the minds of men.

The Lost Glory is a vital work for the 21st Century church and should be read by all who want to understand the sensitive and dangerous nature of music and worship in the life of all mankind. Dave Markee in his simple yet insightful way captures the heart of this subject and communicates the principles that undergird this critical area. David also brings experience and practical history to this issue and masterfully paints a picture that awakens the soul, challenges the intellect and edifies the spirit. It is my hope that as you read *The Lost Glory*, you will not only gain the wisdom and knowledge on these pages, but that you will also see and experience the restoration of the lost glory of God to your life.

Dr Myles Munroe
International author, speaker and broadcaster

David Markee is a gifted musician and pastor with a passion in his heart to restore to the Church the fullness of the glory of God through worship. He makes it very clear that music originates in the heart of God and carries an incredibly influential power, not only to affect the feelings of people, but to open their hearts and prepare them to be on the frontline of the Lord's end-time army.

He speaks of the Church's loss due to its radically fluctuating history of trying to dictate what is holy and acceptable, and the continuing tension that exists between segments of the Church and artists who want to bring creative variety into worship. He insists that our individual preferences as to style are no more than that; God is primarily concerned with the state of the heart of the worshipper, and how the exercise of the musician's anointed gift calls people into the presence of the Lord. David emphasizes the importance of the artist's being made whole in Christ, offering his/her gift to the Lord for redemption.

David also brings to the reader an awareness of the spiritual sensitivity of gifted musicians, and how they can be overwhelmed by the brokenness they sense in people, until they understand what is happening and come into a relationship with Jesus, whereby they lift their burdens to His cross.

All this and much more make this book well worth reading and we heartily commend it.

John and Paula Sandford
Elijah House

There are two kinds of book on any book shelf: those that read like they were written simply because the author was asked to write something, and those that were written because the author couldn't help it – they had to get the book inside them out. I've learned that the second type are the ones worth reading. Dave Markee **had** to write this passionate call to the Church, its leaders and its artists. *The Lost Glory* is a summons to recognize and recover the vital role artistic gifts have to play in revealing God's character and purposes, not only for a hungry Church but for a waiting world.

Steve Chalke
Founding Director, Oasis Trust

David Markee has written a timely book which is calling for Christian artists to once again lead the way in music, art and literature. Yes Lord! May there be a new renaissance!

John Arnott
Senior Pastor
Toronto Airport Christian Fellowship

The result of spreading the gospel is worshippers of Jesus Christ. God is after worshippers for His Son and the Son of God is wanting to draw us near to His Father. David Markee's book will help clear accumulated debris and draw worship from our lives.

Gerald Coates
Speaker, author, broadcaster

'A worshippers heart' – we've used the phrase freely over the last few years. David Markee has been so instrumental in my life, modeling that phrase. In this book, through historic, experiential and biblical perspective, David reveals to the reader the tool to help sort through the 'heart issues' of being a worshipper. The Father heart of worship is vital to the expressive health of each of us, as we were created to worship God 'with our whole hearts'. David Markee shows us all, not only through this book, but in his life by example, a reconciled heart of worship.

Dan Cutrona
President, Kle-Toi Records, Canada

Why oh why didn't we have this 20 years ago? A masterly and anointed narrative written by a man who has experienced the good, bad and ugly of music – both sacred and secular – and is not afraid to say so. This is an important resource for the whole Church. Musicians and artists will be relieved, encouraged and inspired by its contents, and the Church can only know greater blessing.

Steve Hepden
Philos Trust

Foreword

Musicians take heart! Worshippers be encouraged! Dave Markee, a master musician and anointed worship leader has taken on the role of a divine detective. As the 'Scotland Yard' of the spirit, Dave begins tracing the stolen property of God. With dogged determination reminiscent of the lore of Sherlock Holmes, he probes away at the mystery of iniquity. In this book, Dave holds Lucifer in the glaring light of God's Word for our interrogation. By the eternal laws of the Holy Writ he is found guilty. Lucifer, glory thief! Now the process of restoring what was stolen begins. Recognizing divine fingerprints on music, Dave helps us to restore it to its rightful owner and Creator. Music was created by God, for God. The first rebels were heavenly musicians and the restorers must be earthly worshippers.

This book contains a rarity. Theology from a musician. With great wisdom Dave links worship with authority, insight that comes because he is also a successful pastor. With a master musician's skill he harmonizes warfare with worship in the same seamless way that King David shifted between warrior and worshipper. One chapter in particular pulls at the root of jealousy that is so amazingly present among musicians. Before he finishes, right motives are restored to the pursuit of musical excellence in worship.

Whether you agree or not, Dave Markee's credentials insist you listen, and listen well my friend! There is the distilled wisdom of years of music making and worship in this book. All that was lost shall be restored!

Tommy Tenney
September 1999
Louisiana, USA

Preface

'To me it seems as if when God conceived the world, that was poetry; He formed it, and that was sculpture; He colored it, and that was painting; He peopled it with living beings, and that was grand, divine, eternal drama.'   (Emma Stebbins; 1816–1876)

As we begin this new millennium, it's obvious that God is on the move in the arts again. Many prophecies over the last fifteen years or so have borne witness to this fact. In the last four or five years there have also been many prophecies originating from all over the world that say there is a 'new wave' of God coming, and that He is going to put artists, musicians and creative people in the forefront of this move of His Spirit. Given that, I believe with all my heart that this is the right time for this book – absolutely 100%.

The battle for territory

Any Christian with a basic grasp of New Testament theology will know that we are in a spiritual battle. A battle is mostly concerned with gaining or defending territory, a fight for ownership and territorial rights. As Christians we are involved in warfare with principalities and powers that are continually encroaching upon territory that is rightfully ours. We cannot afford to passively accept this state of affairs, but should instead be seeking to take the offensive and reclaim the territory that has been lost, because, in fact, we are actively involved whether we like it or not. The contested 'territory' has even included a battle for the rights to the ownership of creation itself. The atheistic and materialistic evolutionary philosophy that has pervaded western society strongly denies God's ownership of creation, while Christians continue to assert it. This particular battle has raged for hundreds of years and has been heightened more than ever by society's growing desire for a rationalistic, 'pick-and-mix' religion that only embraces the things it finds palatable. The battle for the ownership of creation has also been extended to include the territorial rights of these things called 'music' and 'art' – even of creativity itself. This battle is in the **understanding**; it is taking place largely in the mind, as we will discover shortly. The enemy has so far managed to pollute and darken the thinking of vast sections of the Church, as well as countless creative artists. However, if we are to see a new wave of God's power that will harness the gifts and abilities of such people, called to creative worship, we should not be surprised that these are the very people that the enemy is keen to attack and destroy. Our enemy, satan, hates and detests any God-inspired worship and worshipper – they are a serious threat to the kingdom of darkness.

In Ephesians 1:17 we read this prayer:

> '... that the God of our Lord Jesus Christ, the Father of glory, may give you the Spirit of wisdom and revelation in the knowledge of Him, that the eyes of your understanding being enlightened you may know what is the hope of His calling and what are the riches of the glory of His inheritance in the saints.'

Having our eyes opened to receive a revelation of who Jesus Christ really is, and who we are in Him, is absolutely vital to effective Christianity. Without such revelation it is impossible to make any progress at all, and we will pose no threat to spiritual powers and principalities. This scripture reveals to us by implication a favorite tactic of the enemy, to propagate spiritual blindness and cloud understanding wherever possible. It shows us that much of the battle will take place in the heart, the mind, and the spirit of a person. It is a battle to gain understanding of our true identity in Christ – who we are, and what God has made possible for us. It is also a battle to discover our true purpose in Christ – the realization of what God has planned for our life and the abilities He has given us to use for His glory. Amidst the battle for creativity the Church has suffered heavy losses among its creative warriors. It seems as though we have unwittingly co-operated with the enemy and wounded one another, as well as forgetting how to apply the many creative gifts God has given us to worship Him with. Creative people have been misunderstood, misused and estranged from the Church for many years. The enemy must be very happy about this. He knows only too well the enormous potential for creative worship that could so easily be unlocked and released.

Max McLean said,

> 'Creative men and women are in the church. Some express their art through music ... but others sit quietly alone; waiting to be affirmed, encouraged, supported. They are waiting for the body of Christ to understand and find room for the novel, the film, the play, the masterpiece ruminating within that could reach beyond the subculture and challenge the basic assumptions of our secular age and point the world to the ultimate truth.'

How true, and how sad! My prayer is that God will use this book to reveal the truth to you; to enlighten your mind and quicken your understanding, so that you may know the hope to which you have been called.

Stolen property

Artists and musicians are called to be part of an end-time army, marked by humility and brokenness, which will take back what has been stolen from the Church and the kingdom of God. 1 Samuel chapter 30 tells a wonderful story about King David the warrior. In this story he and his men have been away on a campaign. They return to Ziklag to find that the Amalekites have invaded, taken all their possessions and kidnapped their families. David does a very interesting thing at this point. Usually, when someone steals something from you, your first reaction is to go and get it back **immediately**. However, instead of reacting instinctively, David goes before the Lord and prays, *'Lord, **shall I** go after them?'* God replies, *'Go, you will get everything back.'* Going on a mission to reclaim stolen property because you feel aggrieved and violated is one thing, but to go with a mandate from Almighty God, under His authority, to reclaim what is rightfully yours, is another matter entirely. You plus God is a majority!

So David goes into the Amalekite camp with God's approval and authority. He finds his enemies eating, drinking and rejoicing over what they have taken from him. The Bible says that David attacked them all day and all night and was absolutely determined not to give up until he got everything back. In the same way, I believe that God is raising up an end-time army who will have the same heart and spirit as King David. There will be a spirit in them that will want to go behind enemy lines and persist until they get back everything that has been stolen – music, the arts, entertainment, the media – all the things that have slipped out of the grasp of the Church and have been counterfeited by the enemy. In order to fight this battle, however, these soldiers will have to be battle-fit, well equipped, and know what their armor is. They must be armed with essential military intelligence – knowing their enemy; where he lives; what his strategy is; and where his camp is. I have written this book to try to address some of those issues. Please come with me on this journey.

*'I went to the enemy's camp,
got back what he stole from me...'*
(Traditional chorus)

SECTION 1

Glory Lost

God has been robbed of His inheritance
in creative people.
The battle is on to reclaim them
and bring the glory to God.
He desires to restore true creativity
and worship to His people.
Our heavenly Father desires to heal us,
sanctify us, and help us to discover
our true identity in Christ.
He longs for us to come as little children
and surrender to Him,
so He can reveal to us our true identity.

Chapter 1

The Lost Glory

I have been a musician for 40 years. I was introduced to music by listening to the Ted Heath Big Band on the radio with my father. My dad was a frustrated big band drummer who loved to accompany his broadcasts by playing a pair of hairbrushes on a record cover. I was about 9 years old then, and somehow his passion got into my spirit because I eventually began playing the guitar at the age of 15, took up the bass at 18, and became a professional musician at 19. I am 55 now, and since then have walked, worked, laughed and cried with some of the best and some of the worst in almost every field of music. I started out as a jazz musician, then trained classically at Trinity College of Music, London. Since then, by the grace of God, I've been involved in blues and rock music, films, television, radio and records. I've played on cruise liners and ships, in bars, in clubs and strip joints, in studios, stadiums and concert halls, and for 40 years in this wilderness I have seen and heard musicians and artists express their pain in various ways. This book is aimed primarily at creative people, regardless of their specific discipline, who have found Christ, and yet have not found the fullness of joy in worshipping Him, and also for those who are still searching for meaning in their art and their lives.

The lost glory

There is a deep cry in the heart of every creative person – the frustration of the artist, the sense of being deeply misunderstood and out of place, at odds even with creation itself. It is like being an alien or an exile on the globe. There is a deep longing within – a gut feeling, an almost tantalizing expectation that something indescribably satisfying is yet to come. There is a yearning in the heart and the mind of the artist for something that is not yet, and occasionally an almost prophetic sense that one day we will step into it, or perhaps simply stumble upon it round the next bend.

Anyone who has ever been involved in creative things has almost certainly felt at times like they were perhaps a little bit mad – or at the very least assumed others were thinking it of them. But we are not really, because sometimes – just occasionally – we catch a glimpse of something divine, like a curtain being drawn back just for a second. We are privileged for a moment in time to experience paradise – we are in it, and it is coming down to us. We can almost see and hear the sounds of heaven, as the inspirational genius of the Holy Spirit connects with our God-given gifts, creating in us a unique worshipping ability – and this is real! It is a time when we are able to be ourselves and worship God in our way, as only we can.

These are the times that creative people live for and feed on, when heaven comes to visit. It seems possible in everything we do – play, sing, paint, or create – to have the hallmark of heaven on it. When it happens it is as natural as the breath of life flowing through us. The divine connection is made; somebody throws the cosmic switch and everything works as it should. Creativity is no longer a struggle. We know what we want to do; we are clear minded, and everything we do works!

Sadly, all too soon the curtain is closed once more, leaving us breathless, and the ordinariness we have been accustomed to returns. We are back in what people call the 'normal' world; feeling again at odds with creation – aliens once more. It is almost like a hand reached down to us, took us from the earth, and just when we thought we had reached our true destination, let us go.

What I have just described has happened to almost every artist, musician, dancer or painter I have ever met. They all talk of a tremendous frustration in their hearts. Sadly, many look everywhere for satisfaction and completion except to the Creator of creativity Himself.

A conspiracy theory

The enemy has fabricated a grand conspiracy. There is a big lie here that attempts to convince us we can achieve satisfaction through art and creativity itself. That if we can only live life with this sense of creativity flowing through us, then everything will be OK. But tremendous frustration comes when we try to find complete fulfillment in our art. Nevertheless, many constantly try. Some people grow sick of waiting and give themselves to other things. I heard recently that a musician I greatly admired had died of a heart attack at a very young age. The 'high' he experienced during these 'divine moments' was so rare for him that the only satisfaction he could get out of 'normal' life was through sniffing cocaine. He was desperately looking for satisfaction and meaning, and was immensely frustrated. Scores of stories of similar tragedies can be told of artists down through the ages. Creative person after creative person has fallen prey to sickness, sin, accidental death, and sometimes even suicide through attempting to deal with this tremendous pain by themselves.

Artists will never find what they are looking for in their art. I have learned that trying to gain affirmation from one's giftedness just does not work because in order to achieve this, one has to aspire to perfection – to be consistently improving and never making any mistakes – that would bring satisfaction and affirmation, but it is an impossible ideal. Eugene Delacroix said, 'Artists who seek perfection in everything are those who cannot attain it in anything.' It is all part of the 'satisfaction vibe' that musicians get stuck on – an obsession with striving for perfection that always leaves the person unsatisfied and unhappy about the present level of ability they have. When they reach for this illusion and fail to grasp it, it usually results in depression. I was no exception. My wife used to say to me, 'You walk around with a portable black cloud over your head, even in the good times.' It was a puzzle to me, until one day, during prayer, God showed me what the problem was.

The Lord reminded me of a time when I was 13 years old. I was sitting on a couch with my Mum and Dad (one of the rare occasions I can remember that ever happening). My Dad asked me, 'What do you want to do with your life?' and I told him that I wanted to be a musician. He laughed at me and ridiculed me and eventually it became so painful that I ended up just hugging my guitar to my chest. Instead of receiving the affirmation I needed, I received ridicule, and I looked to my music, represented by my guitar, to give me the comfort I sought. It was a deep, wounding experience and God showed me that an unhealthy spiritual bonding had occurred. Going to music for comfort actually became a life habit for me. Even in adult life, if I had a disagreement with anyone, I would go and play my bass and feel better. As a professional musician however, it became a problem. If I had a good session where everything turned out well, I would be happy because everyone was pleased, I was affirmed, and I felt good about myself. If I had a bad day, however, it would have the opposite effect. Sometimes I did not have what the client was looking for. In truth they were looking for something that nobody could give them. This made me very depressed, sometimes for days. When you reach this point it is easy to begin a downward spiral, because the very music you seek to take comfort from has become your enemy – now even your art has let you down and caused you pain.

When the Lord revealed this 'buried' memory from childhood to me, I knew I had to break the ungodly soul-ties and bondage that were there and tell my heavenly Father that from now on, He would have to be the one source of my affirmation and comfort. When I think of the way that this bondage had defiled my natural gift I realized why I had always felt that I was fighting myself.

God has allowed the events of my life to shape my understanding of the frustration of the artist, and I want to share these thoughts with you. First, and most importantly, I want to say that real satisfaction comes only from knowing Jesus, and allowing Him to show you the Father. God truly is **my** Father, He was the One who created me and gave me a burning passion for creativity. Salvation is not to be found in art or creativity, but only in the person of Jesus Christ. I believe the only thing that can really satisfy any artist is an intimate relationship with Him and a knowledge of His glory. 'Glory' is a good word. To live **in** the glory of God, and have the glory of God **in us**, is glorious! It is the only thing that can ever truly satisfy any human being, because that was always God's plan. Secondly, we must recognize the nature of the problem we have as creative people. The battle we wage is to overcome the lack of understanding, lack of knowledge, and lack of revelation of the nature of creative people, that has created so much confusion. Hurting artists have often retreated to 'hide' in their art and have turned their gifts inwards, instead of using the talents God gave them to reflect His glory outwards to others. As a result, they have remained hurting and misunderstood, while others have failed or refused to see that their God-given talents would flourish under His direction. Only when we come out of hiding and allow God to shape and direct us through an intimate relationship with Him will we be truly free to express ourselves fully.

The purpose of this book is to 'give permission' to the Church and many frustrated artists and musicians to do and be what God has already said 'Yes' to. In these days the Lord is knocking at the door of various long-held and erroneous teachings and 'doctrines' that really amount to no more than personal preferences, cultural differences or misunderstood truths, which have succeeded in preventing both the Church and the artist from reflecting God's glory as they should. This book also aims to show that the road to fulfillment – where all our gifts and abilities are fully used by God and we live in His glory – must pass through the territories of healing, of discovering one's destiny in Christ, and becoming like children, trusting and releasing to God all that we so desperately cling to.

This book is the result of a 40-year personal pilgrimage both as a pagan and a committed Christian. It is inevitably a compilation of personal revelation and that which I have learned from both Christian and non-Christian men and women, authors and teachers, who have helped to shape my own thinking over the years. Because I am a musician, naturally many of the illustrations I use are musical ones! But I trust that you will be able to learn from the broad principles outlined, and apply them to your own specific calling. I earnestly hope and pray that this book will go some way to helping you come to terms with the creative gift that God has given you. Each chapter ends with a *Selah* – a term used throughout the Psalms which means literally: 'Think about it'! Please consider the following thoughts and pray through them for yourself.

Selah...

'Bad will be the day for every man when he becomes absolutely content with the life that he is living, with the thoughts that he is thinking, with the deeds that he is doing, when there is not forever beating at the doors of his soul some great desire to do something larger, which he knows that he was meant and made to do because he is still, in spite of it all, a child of God.'

(Philip Brooks; 1835–1893)

Thank the Lord for His creative gift in you. Fully accept it from the Father. Tell Him that you will respect it, honor it, and do your very best to make it better, to increase it, and to plant it so that it may increase and be effective. Make a decision to allow God to speak to you, to guide you and work in you, so that you will discover more about your destiny in Him.

Chapter 2

What On Earth Went Wrong?

Creativity: Who owns the copyright?

The history and development of music, and the historical attitude of the Church toward it, is of great concern to me. What on earth went wrong? It's clear that something did. Throughout history there has been an uneasy tension between the Church and those who have sought to bring creative variety to its worship. And yet the Bible points to a very different scenario. Consider the Bible itself for a moment. Among other things, it is surely the greatest 'worship-book' the world has ever known. There are songs, poems, meditations, prayers and prose – arguably the greatest ever written. With such variety at our disposal, how can worship become routine?

Throughout Church history there have been differences of opinion about the use of music in worship. There has been great controversy over its validity, and even a question mark over the need for music in the Church at all. Theologians have hotly debated this issue for years, but winds of change are blowing again. The Church desperately needs a fresh understanding of the biblical importance of the ministry of worship (as a whole and including musical worship), and creative people need a good answer for the theologians who would try to persuade us otherwise. I believe the heart of the issue is that we need to think again about who owns creativity. What is the purpose of it? Why do we have it? Did it originate with man or someone else?

Before we complicate this debate by discussing styles or forms, let's answer this question: who owns the copyright?

There are only three possibilities. It either originated with God, the devil or man. For example, Scripture suggests that music originated in the very heart of God. It says in the Bible that right at the dawn of creation, the angels sang and there was heavenly music (Job 38:4–7). God created the planets and set them all in orbit. He set the stars in the heavens and composed His incredible universe. Creation itself is a wonderful, moving, sound and light show. It is the most wonderful thing you could ever think of. There is a melody and a harmony in creation itself that reveals God's musical heart.

We must also look back at real historical events surrounding the dawn of creation that reveal God's original intentions for the use of music. Scripture teaches that God created the angelic hosts of heaven and they became a heavenly choir that sang at creation. Many Bible scholars believe that Lucifer was the original identity of satan before he fell (see Ezekiel 28 and Isaiah 14). Having said that, there are other theories regarding these scriptures that we should briefly review.

Isaiah 14:12–15 is a key passage in the debate:

> *'How art thou fallen from heaven, O Lucifer, son of the morning! How art thou cut down to the ground, which didst weaken the nations! For thou hast said in thine heart, I will ascend into heaven, I will exalt my throne above the stars of God: I will sit also upon the mount of the congregation, in the sides of the north: I will ascend above the heights of the clouds; I will be like the most High. Yet thou shalt be brought down to hell, to the sides of the pit.'*
>
> (King James Version)

Technically, the name 'Lucifer' is not from the Hebrew Bible. It found its way into Scripture via the King James version of the Bible through Middle English, Old English and Latin (the Vulgate) as an interpretation of the Hebrew word *helel*. The Latin literally means 'light-bearing (one)' from *lux* (light) and *ferre* (to bear). The Hebrew word *helel* is derived from *halal*, meaning to shine (different from another Hebrew root which uses the same letters – *halal*, meaning 'to praise'). Transliterated, the phrase referring to Lucifer in Isaiah 14:12, in Hebrew would read, *'O Helel, son of the dawn/morning . . . '*

The derivative, *helel*, occurs as a proper name only once in the Old Testament (here in Isaiah 14:12). Otherwise, it occurs six times in the Old Testament in poetic or mythical settings (Job 29:3; 31:26; Isaiah 60:19; Joel 2:31) or settings of judgment (Isaiah 13:13; Ezekiel 32:7; Joel 2:10) and is always connected with the sense of the shining of heavenly bodies (the sun, moon, and stars).

One theory is that the description in Isaiah 14 bears similarities to a Canaanite myth of a dawn-goddess who attempted to ascend to heaven and was sentenced to be thrown down to Sheol forever. 'Evidence for this point of view may be found in the words *har moed* – mount of assembly, and the name *tsaphon* – mountain of the north, both resembling the Canaanite mountain of the gods (a common motif in the Ancient Near East)' (*Theological Wordbook of the Old Testament*). If these allusions to ancient Canaanite superstition are correct, then in this Old Testament passage, the Lord is essentially mocking their pagan gods whilst stating the truth that only He is Lord over all. But how typical of our enemy, satan, trying to pass himself off as some ancient mythical deity in order to throw a smokescreen around his true identity and purpose!

Another view is that, '...the passage seems clearly to be a taunt song against the king of Babylon in Isaiah's time (14:3), who later in the Bible is used as a prefiguration of the "beast" who will lead "Babylon" in the last days (Revelation 13:4; 17:3)' (*NIV Study Bible*).

My firm belief however, given the prophetic nature of the book of Isaiah, which often foreshadows future events whilst commenting on current ones, is that none of these possible interpretations ought to be thought of as mutually exclusive. Hebrew is a rich language. It doesn't always mean one, and only one thing. In this case Isaiah is prophesying against a human ruler (the king of Babylon), as well as against the principalities and powers behind that ruler (the Canaanite or Babylonian mythologies), **and** giving insight into the character, nature and fate of the chief antagonist of God's will in the heavenly realm, satan, who wanted to be 'like the Most High' and who tempted Adam and Eve. His malignant personality was behind the activities of this earthly ruler.

Similarly, Charles Feinberg, commenting on the Ezekiel 28 passage, said:

> 'Ezekiel ... appeared to have the situation of his day in mind with his attention riveted upon the ruler of Tyre ... but as he viewed the thoughts and ways of that monarch, he clearly discerned behind him the motivating force and personality who was impelling him in his opposition to God. In short he saw the work and activity of satan, whom the king of Tyre was emulating...' [1]

Dr W.A. Criswell also confirms this view by saying:

> 'This lamentation directed toward the king of Tyre (Ezekiel 28:12–19) defies explanation unless an allusion is being made to that malignant spiritual being called "satan" or the "devil", for whom the king of Tyre becomes a type ... Sometime prior to the creation of the natural order, satan became vain about his beauty and position, and his heart became rebellious against God. Apparently, he was able to secure a considerable following among the angels, resulting in the expulsion of himself and his followers from heaven (Luke 10:18, 2 Peter 2:4, Jude 6, Revelation 12:4).' [2]

If satan and Lucifer were the same person, then the Bible suggests that he was heaven's choir leader. His original identity as the *son of the morning* reveals a strong connection to the dawn of creation itself. He was an anointed cherub with a distinct anointing for ministry. Ezekiel 28 reveals him as the covering cherub – covering the throne of God on the mountain of God. He was created perfect in beauty and was full of wisdom – the heavenly archangel in Eden, the paradise of God. He was clothed as a priest with precious stones in his garments, made to reflect God's glory as the 'light-bearer', and was the most beautiful of all God's creation. The King James Version of the Bible says that he had the workmanship of tabrets and pipes actually inside him the day he was created. In other words he literally **was** music and God was able to sing through this archangel and create music through him. This was his ministry – the very breath of God would come through him and create beautiful sounds. God would play him like an instrument, but he became proud of his own beauty and it corrupted him, He wanted to keep all the beautiful worship for himself. He forgot that God had given him his gifts and abilities.

Job 38:4–7 says that the morning stars sang together and all the sons of God shouted. If we accept that the morning stars and the sons of God are the angelic hosts in heaven, then clearly singing and shouting took place at the time of creation. There was beautiful singing and very loud shouting. The purpose of this music was to give glory to God and rejoice in the wonder of His creative power as He 'assembled' the universe. Music and worship were inextricably linked from the very beginning.

Selah...

Holy Spirit of God, please show me any way in which the 'light' in me has been corrupted. Help me to use my gifts and abilities to glorify God, and never for my own satisfaction.

Three archangels

Besides Lucifer, there were two other chief archangels in heaven – Gabriel and Michael. All three had their own particular ministries. Gabriel was the archangel of communication – the messenger. Michael was the prince of Israel – the warrior, and Lucifer – the worship leader! These three archangels had charge of all the heavenly hosts between them and clearly each had different functions. When Lucifer was cast down from heaven because of his pride, he took with him a third of the angelic hosts. There is a good case for suggesting that the third he took with him were the ones he was already working with – the musical ones! The Bible says he was full of wisdom, beauty and music. He clearly knew and understood the power of music. I believe that the ones he had been conducting, the heavenly choir,

were the ones that fell with him. God kicked him out and the
choir left with him. It makes theological sense.

So is there any music at all now in heaven? An examina-
tion of Scripture reveals a strange fact. Whilst there is
definitely singing and shouting, thunder and lightning in
heaven, the only instruments to be found are the harps
played by the twenty-four elders who sing a new song in
Revelation.

> *'...round the throne were voices, thunder and lightning.'*
> (Revelation 4:5)

> *'...four living creatures, they never cease to **sing** "Holy,
> Holy, Holy."'*   (Revelation 4:8)

> *'...twenty-four elders fell down before the Lamb. Each
> of the elders had a harp and they had golden bowls full of
> incense, the prayers of God's people. They were **singing** a
> new song.'*   (Revelation 4:8–9)

It is important to qualify these statements in Revelation.
One strand of thought regarding the 'vision' unfolded by the
Apostle John is that the chapters from 4 onwards speak of
future events yet to take place. Another is that the whole
of the book describes past, present and future events, all
seamlessly interwoven – the classical view of interpreting
prophecy. This being so, it is hard for us to pinpoint the exact
timing of these events. What we can be certain of however, is
that throughout Scripture 'singing' is referred to as the major
form of worship taking place in heavenly realms, rather than
instrumental music.

We must think further. There have been reliable reports
here on earth by people who claimed to hear the sounds of
angels joining in with their worship – a host of angelic voices
singing wonderfully, albeit in very high pitches and tones
almost exceeding the range audible by the human ear. For
many years now, hungry musicians have prayed, 'Lord, let us
hear the sounds of heaven,' presumably so they could
reproduce those sounds on earth. If God did allow us such a
privilege, according to the Revelation account, we would

hear thunder, lightning, singing and shouting, but little instrumentation. Think about it, a band of twenty-four harpists would only fill the bottom level of the stage of the Albert Hall, London, even if the harps encompassed a wide range of sound – from baritone to piccolo. Would it be glorious and extravagant enough to cover the throne of Almighty God in heaven? However, there is plenty of music going on down here on earth. Lots of it! Hundreds and hundreds of creative artists are doing wonderful things with music right now.

Was music cast down to earth along with Lucifer? Has God lost His covering? I believe so, and also I believe that God is listening hard for pure, Spirit and truth music to rise up from the earth. His plan was always to have His throne covered with worship, and He lost His worship band when the angels fell. As satan has planned and schemed how to attack God's creation – mankind – God has purposed to use mankind to become the worship covering around His throne instead of Lucifer, thereby publicly humiliating him in heaven and making a further example of him, just as he was humiliated when Christ defeated him at the cross.

So, when God had to start over again with a new worship band, He started with us. This is why the ministry of worship is so vitally important in the Church, and why God is taking so much time, trouble and effort to encourage us to take hold of our rightful ownership of it. This is also why satan has fought so hard at keeping his grip on music, musicians and creative people in general. The Church is the only agency on earth with the authority from God to go and get them back. It is our job to cover the throne of God with beautiful sounds of worship, then He will inhabit the praises of His people

The Bible is clear in stating that the gifts and the calling of God are irrevocable (Romans 11:29). Once He gives you a gift He does not snatch it back. This explains why we sometimes see people with tremendous ministries living a bad life and yet still walking in the anointing. Lucifer did not forfeit his ministry of music – but he did corrupt it. He turned it round and now uses it against God. He contaminated it and today it is one of his most effective weapons, used to draw people away from the truth and wisdom only to be found in the

Lord Jesus Christ. It has been said, if you want to corrupt a nation, first of all corrupt its music and art. The enemy always knew this and it has formed the spearhead of his offensive strategies.

God desires a people who will worship Him in Spirit and in truth. As we do that we will become prophetic warriors for Him. The enemy always attacks a prophet and there is a spirit abroad in the world that seeks to shut the prophetic down. To a large degree, the enemy has succeeded in using misunderstanding and ignorance in the Church to help him do this. That is why we, as creative people, must know who we are, understand our creative gifts from God, know what we are armed with and see where we are going. We must be clear about what we believe and what the Bible says about the role we play. Music belongs to God. He invented it and He has given us the gift of creating it and using it to worship Him.

Selah...

'The poor and needy search for water; but there is none. Their tongues are parched with thirst. But I the Lord will answer them; I, the God of Israel, will not forsake them. I will make rivers flow on barren heights, and springs within the valleys. I will turn the desert into pools of water, and the parched ground into springs. I will put in the dessert the cedar and acacia, the myrtle and the olive. I will set pines in the wasteland, the fir and the cypress together, so that people may see and know, may consider and understand, that the hand of the Lord has done this, that the Holy One of Israel has created it.'   (Isaiah 41:17–20)

Lord help me to see, know, consider and understand the call You have placed on my life. Amen

Greek influence or biblical truth?

If you have ever attended a lecture on the history of music in Western culture you will have seen that all through the ages men and women of learning have looked back to

Greece when trying to identify the origins of music. Many of the attitudes of Western civilization towards music and the behavior of creative people can be traced back to Greek thought. Also, because the Church has historically failed to assert its legal ownership of the creative arts, the influence of secular culture upon 'Church music' has been insidious.

The Greeks loved knowledge and carried out extensive studies on the nature of music and sound. Greek thought and mythology ascribed a divine origin to music. They thought that their gods had conceived music and gave names to the 'inventors': Apollo, Amphion and Orpheus.[3] In this ancient world they recognized the spiritual power of music. People thought that it could heal sickness, purify the soul and mind, and work miracles in the realm of nature. Basically they had some things right in their assumptions – they were just confused about the Inventor! The Bible tells us that indeed Saul's madness was healed while David played his harp; the walls of Jericho fell when the people walked around them blowing their trumpets, and the enemies of Jehoshaphat were thrown into confusion by worship. God can use music powerfully to accomplish His plans.

During the lifetime of Greek poet Homer (credited as author of Greek mythical epics the *Iliad* and *Odyssey*), it was common to sing poems at banquets depicting battles. From earliest times music was a part of religious ceremony. The singing of poetry accompanied by reed pipes was used in the worship of Dionysus.[4] It is thought that from this the concept of Greek drama was developed, and this in turn led to the development of many virtuoso artists. Even at this very early stage a controversy began that still rages in the Church to this day. Some people would say that the most important thing was the spirit of the music being played, and others would say that it was essential to be accomplished on one's instrument. These two camps were always debating whether it was better to be a good **technical** musician or a good **feeling** musician. Surely a worshipper who has skill, who has an intimate, love relationship with the Lord Jesus brings greater glory to God. It's about time we had both!

Sound familiar? Allow me a small digression. While we're discussing it, I would like to say that there is nothing wrong with striving for excellence in worship. God delights in excellence – just look at the many wonderful colors He paints in a sunset, or a beautiful flower. And we are called to reflect His glory too! There are elements within the Church that seem afraid to use excellence, extravagance, or performance simply for their own sake. Yet God entertains us with the staggering abundance of nature, so it's OK for us to entertain others too. We shouldn't be ashamed of excellence. Please, do not let us marginalize countless artists, poets, dancers and musicians by 'banning' the element of gifted excellence from our theology of worship. The problem is never with excellence – it is always with the inability that artists have, from time to time, to give the glory back to God. Our problems begin when, as artists, we receive worship for ourselves and fail to give God the credit for the effective use of our gifts. That doesn't mean we should continually apologize for our gifts or put ourselves down, but we simply seek always to honor Jesus. True humility, someone has said, is drawing oneself up to one's full height, fully acknowledging all our gifts and abilities, and realizing how small is our greatness compared to God. Also, if you practice false humility, God does not get any return on His investment, so be as good as you can be for Him!

Let's resume our study and continue to think about the influence Greek culture has exerted on us. The Greeks were totally absorbed with the pursuit of truth and beauty. They loved knowledge and they discussed and criticized every form of art in order to try to understand more about it. The effect it has had upon us, because we absorbed their philosophy into our Western culture, is that we too in the west have become very critical and more concerned with rationalizing and debating than appreciating beauty for its own sake. We have also lost sight of the true origin of music which always had its roots in worship. In fact, the history of our Western art, music, and modern culture rightfully begins with the Christian Church. It is said in some Jewish synagogues even today, and believed in the Jewish mind, that God's people were the original genius musicians and artists, because God had touched their minds and their hearts in a spectacular way. This is the Church's true and great heritage, but satan himself has vehemently resisted it. Throughout history he has conceived various programs designed to drive creativity and art from the Church.

So then, the purpose of music has always been to express our worship to the Creator. Remember the morning stars singing before the throne of God at the dawn of creation? These fallen angels are now the principalities and powers that are raised against us, and they are still able to sing their song of creation. The gifts and call of God are irrevocable, so these angels are **still** singing. Think about this for a moment. What makes a musical sound? It is the vibration of moving air. One of satan's titles is the *'prince of the power of the air'* (Ephesians 2:2).[5] He knows how to corrupt the airwaves perfectly! He has been using music to undermine truth in society and all our cultural value systems. Perhaps you think that a strong statement? And yet, every second of the day airwaves the world over are filled with hypnotic rhythms accompanied by lyrics that preach a humanistic, atheist, relativist gospel that is drip-fed constantly into its' inhabitants souls.

> *'The god of this age has blinded the minds of unbelievers, so that they cannot see the light of the gospel of the glory of Christ, who is the image of God.'*   (2 Corinthians 4:4)

The world is busy singing the same 'creation anthem' as the fallen angels.

It is time for Christians to realize that we have been robbed and deceived! Not only have we been fed the lie that either the devil or man originated music, rather than God; we have also fallen prey to a conspiracy spread around by the enemy that Christian artists are somehow second-class citizens and cannot use art and music as effectively as our enemy. This is the big lie – that as Christian artists we are not as good as those in 'the world' who are singing this song of creation. Most Christian artists will immediately identify with that concept and will more than likely have felt 'second-class' themselves at some point. And yet the Bible insists that God has revealed things to us that angels long to look into. They long to understand the things that we know and look into the things that we, as born-again children of God, have seen. Surely we have a song to sing that the angels know nothing of!

When someone is born, they receive the gifts of God as natural abilities. Whether you are a Christian or not you can still play the guitar. You don't have to be a Christian to play the drums. You don't have to be a Christian to paint or write or sculpt or play the piano. The creative gift is there. It is a gift given by God at the dawn of your creation. However, unless you have been redeemed by the blood of the Lamb you will only be able to sing the same song as those fallen angels. Unless you have been saved by the Lord Jesus Christ and have come into a relationship with the Living God, you will never be able to sing a better song. The world is full of talented, gifted artists, but how many are struggling to make sense of the world and having little or no success. As a child of God you have a better song to sing and the power of God's Holy Spirit to help you sing it.

As a Christian artist or musician, you are part of the only company of people on the face of the earth uniquely qualified to worship God. You are not second best. You have the potential to rise up and sing, act, compose and reflect God's glory. This is the restoration of glory – the thing that satisfies the heart of the creative person. That is why it is so important for creative people to worship the giver and not the gift. This is completion, this is your destiny – the creative use of your gift under the anointing of God. This is what you were born for. Lucifer knows this because he is music and art and is still full of carnal cleverness which used to be wisdom. But the ownership of art, music and all forms of creativity always did and always will belong to God. He is the rightful owner, and part of our inheritance in Christ is to rediscover how our God-given gifts can be fully utilized in worshipping Him. Despite every attempt of the enemy to rob the Church of these powerful tools, they remain and are rightfully ours. Let us seek to harness the immense power lying dormant within the Body of Christ and rise up in warfare until we see the lost glory restored.

> **Selah...**
>
> *'What is to reach the heart must come from above; if it does not come from thence, it will be nothing but notes, body without spirit.'*   (Ludwig Van Beethoven; 1770–1827)

Notes

1. Feinberg, Charles Lee. *The Prophecy of Ezekiel: The Glory of the Lord.* Chicago, Moody Press, 1969.

2. Criswell, Dr W.A., Ed., *The Believers Study Bible, New King James Version,* Nashville, Thomas Nelson Publishers, 1991.

3. Apollo – in Greek mythology was primarily a god of prophecy and a gifted musician; Amphion was also reputed to be a great musician. Orpheus was by legend a poet and musician 'touched' by the gods to the extent that he had no rival among mortals – so much so that even nature became subdued at his playing.

4. Dionysus – Orphism developed as a mystic cult of ancient Greece from the writings of Orpheus; they centered on the worship of Dionysus, the god of wine, drama, and orgiastic religion celebrating the power and fertility of nature.

5. This title for satan carries the meaning that he is one who influences the mood and manner of society, globally and within each culture – Footnotes, *Spirit Filled Life Bible*, New King James Version.

Chapter 3

The Death and Restoration of Music

God likes music loud! (as well as soft!) Music has a forte as well as a pianissimo – it's called dynamics! And just as music has an endless range of tones, textures and colors, our worship should too. God is equally delighted with the loud and vibrant as well as the soft and intimate. Imagine yourself in the midst of the most awesome worship service ever. It is described in Chapter 4 of the book of Revelation as the Apostle John is astounded by an incredible vision of the throne room of heaven. There was thunder and lightning, various amazing creatures worshipping the Lord night and day, and it all took place in front of a mirrored sea. It must have been so loud – like turning the amplifiers up to way past 12! I remember that the first thing I wanted to do when I was saved was worship God. As a musician that was the highest thing I could do. God is most delighted when we offer Him the spontaneous, unpremeditated response of our hearts in worship. That is worshipping in spirit and truth.

Everything we discover about biblical history and the revealed nature of God points to His desire for spontaneous, creative, extravagant worship – full of variety and prophetic utterance. We have already spoken about a spirit in the earth that desperately wants to shut down the prophetic, and one thing that is really effective in releasing the prophetic is music. Even early Christians knew this. The Jewish historian Flavius Josephus records that even as Christians were being thrown to the lions in the arena, you could hear them

singing above the roars. This must at least have unnerved
their captors, perhaps even terrified them secretly.

Christians throughout history have always expressed
worship to God through song. In fact, our sole purpose in
life (putting aside all the secondary purposes that we often
give pre-eminence to) is 'to glorify God and ... enjoy Him
forever.'[1] It is clear that worship is for everyone, and everyone should always be worshipping. However, church history
tells another story – one where liberty and variety rarely
characterized church worship.

There was a great controversy around the third century
over whether the Psalms alone should be used in music, or
whether people should be allowed to compose hymns. Some
said these songs were sacrilegious and unholy. Around
AD 354, John Chrysostom[2] warned people against the use
of instruments, saying there was no need for them or for
trained voices in church. The rot had started to set in. 200
years later, Bishop Gregory rejected the concept of congregational singing, saying it should be restricted to the choir. He
founded a school for religious music in Rome and sent all the
graduates out to teach the same thing. In essence he was
teaching people that creativity and worship were for an elite
few. He released people all over Europe to teach these
principles and this was only 500 years after the death of
Christ. This is part of the heritage we, the 20th Century
Church, have inherited.

In AD 563 the Council of Braga forbade all singing
except the Psalms of David. Several hundred years later we
entered the period of history known as the Dark Ages, called
by some the Babylonian captivity. The song of the heart that
could be heard above the roar of the lions in the Coliseum
had been virtually shut down. By this time, the main system
operating in the Church was one of a formal clergy. The
congregation was told what to believe and what to do.
Worship was an exercise in listening. A few people tried to
stand against this and were terribly persecuted. Musical
instruments were ruled out totally in church, even though
up until that point they had been welcomed. Compare
this to the scenario in King David's time. He utilized some
700 musicians in one single band! The biblical standard of

extravagant offerings of praise and worship to God had been forgotten and neglected by the Church. In the light of such radical biblical examples, it is hard to understand where people got such ideas.

When musical instruments were kicked out of the Church, they flourished outside, and so the 14th Century became a period when new instruments were invented and developed. For the first time orchestras were formed with strings, wood-wind and percussion of all different types. Violins, harps, psalteries, big drums, chimes, cymbals, bagpipes, reeds, horns and flutes – all are mentioned in the Bible. They called the church organ the king of all instruments and yet it was not allowed to be played in many churches! Even though outside tremendous creativity – the song of creation – was being poured out, the doors of the Church remained firmly closed.

This art form marked a redevelopment and resurgence of Greek thought. The Greeks had established music in theatre and developed it into an art form. Because the Church kicked music out and musical instruments were not used to worship the Creator, the art form of music found its expression elsewhere. Thus began the Church's Babylonian captivity.

The cavalry showed up in the form of the Reformation of 1517 to 1600 when the Lord began to release the Church from bondage. As well as bringing renewal to many other aspects of the Church, music began to be restored. Martin Luther, credited as being the father of the Reformation, played a vital role in the restoration of music. Others had come before him and kept the flame alight, but this tremendous man of God gave music the thrust that it needed. He gave the Church an enormous kick! Martin Luther not only gave the German people the Bible in their own language, he also gave them Christian songs in their own language. The German people were (and, I believe, still are) incredibly important in the restoration of music and art into the Church. They were the recipients of the first wave to release the Church from captivity. I believe another reformation is coming. Currently we see all over the world, pockets of spirit-filled artists gathering and seeking to serve God with their gifts.

Luther was a musician and a composer of hymns and he encouraged others to do the same. The printing press had just been invented which facilitated the wide distribution of Bibles, handbooks and also songsheets. Even so, the opposition remained fierce. People who were in possession of Luther's hymnbooks and Bibles were imprisoned, tortured and put to death. Up to that point the Catholic Church of Rome was the only recognized church and Luther thought the church was far too solemn. He contended for beauty, melody and joy. He was a man filled with the Holy Spirit. He said an amazing thing, that theology was second only to music. Still church leaders were in turmoil because they had been taught that music was very sensual. Luther, however, used German folk tunes and popular songs and put suitable words to glorify God with them. He also defined music as an art form and often spoke about the need for excellence in church music. He upheld the right of musicians to have an adequate and assured income from Church sources (modern Church take note!). The age of patronage started to return. A song by Luther called 'A Mighty Fortress is our God' became the battle song of the Reformation.

An equally influential figure in the Reformation was John Calvin. He was a French theologian who claimed that the Bible, not the Church, was the source of all spiritual authority. However, he differed doctrinally from Luther in the area of arts and music. He encouraged congregational singing, a point in his favor, but strongly disapproved of people composing hymns, insisting that only the Psalms of David should be sung. He also forbade instrumental music in the churches of Geneva. He opposed the introduction of singing with harmony and taught that instrumental music was only tolerated in Israel under the Law because the nation was in infancy. In commenting on Psalm 92 with musical instruments he speaks of these things as being shadows of a departed dispensation – in other words that musical instruments were only intended for God's ancient people. Based upon this proposition, his followers felt it necessary to destroy church organs, removing them en masse from churches and melting them down for the metal. Calvin knew the emotional power of music but he feared it and had distaste for organs, hymns and part-singing in church music. He denied the ability of the Holy Spirit to enable us to worship God in new ways and so he limited the Church again. Sadly, throughout history personal preferences have been taught as if they were biblical doctrine.

Later on, between 1600 to 1800 in the post reformation period, there was a revival of music in the Church again. No matter what the enemy or the organized Church seemed to do to the contrary, God's purpose would not be thwarted. One after another, people emerged throughout history who each played their part. Isaac Watts, the famous hymn writer, maintained that the Psalms were just a Hebrew book and said many of the psalms were not written in the spirit of the New Testament worshipper. He had his own ideas and his own agenda, but nevertheless he started a revival. The Moravians were the first people in America to allow the use of musical instruments in their services. John Huss (circa 1372–1415) used violins, clarinets and trombones his meetings. Brothers John and Charles Wesley gave tremendous impetus to the writing and singing of hymns.

Each generation influenced the next. The Wesleys were greatly influenced by Isaac Watts and the Moravians, who wrote very joyful and triumphant hymns. The Wesleys wrote over 6000 hymns between them. They helped to ensure that the singing of hymns was securely cemented as part of Christian worship. Revivals in America led by Charles Finney, Jonathan Edwards and George Whitfield during the 1700s also gave their weight to the singing of Isaac Watts hymns. The problem that remained however was still the use of musical instruments, and continued to be a very controversial subject. Early Baptists and Presbyterians refused to adopt musical instruments and early Methodists were very slow to accept instrumental music.

So we come to about the 1800s when William Booth, an Anglican filled with the Holy Spirit, founded the Salvation Army because of his passion to see lost souls saved. He understood the modern day culture and could be seen as a 'son of Issachar' – someone who understood the signs of the times.[3] His motto was 'Go for souls and go for the worst ones.' He wanted to take the gospel where no one dared to go – to the bars and clubs, the red light districts – and reach the lowest of the lowest of the low. The Salvation Army developed their own hymn-book and got the idea of forming a band after seeing a Presbyterian group with brass instruments holding a meeting on the street. William Booth thought this was a great idea and formed a band to attract a crowd. They went out on to the streets, rattled tambourines, clapped, shouted and worshipped. It was very exuberant praise, and you can imagine what that did to people. Until then all they had been used to was a meeting with no music at all, or very solemn church music with the singing of hymns or psalms. All of a sudden there were these 'lunatics' on the streets praising God. Just as Luther did, Booth took the popular songs of the day and put Christian words to them. That is how he communicated the message of God's salvation. At last, music started to be welcomed back into the Church's culture.

Even though on various different levels instrumental music has found its way back, we are still having a battle. Ever since rock music has become a popular idiom there has been a fiercely contested debate about whether it is from God or the devil. The debate has seen ridiculous extremes. A friend of mine actually belonged to a church where the worship leader would not play the black notes of the piano, would not play in a minor key, and if he had ever played a blues scale, would probably have been excommunicated by the elders! Why? Because more than we would care to believe the Church is still entrenched in Greek thought, bowing to and empowering worthless superstition. We are still teaching and preaching the doctrine of personal preference. The Greeks believed that certain musical scales or modes had an almost magical effect, and so I believe we once again trace the root of our paranoia to Greek thought and cultural influence. I still hear Christians today saying things like, 'There is no minor key in heaven' or 'There is no discord in heaven'. They still say 'We are not having drums in church because they are demonic.' Please, give me a break! Go back to the textbook and look again. Asaph, King David's right-hand man was a percussionist (1 Chronicles 16:5). God created the whole spectrum of music and gave all of it to us to use in our worship.

No musically educated person can possibly say, 'You can't use this note alongside that one.' All the notes belong to God! There is nothing demonic about them. Maybe your ears don't like certain chords or notes that seem dissonant, but there is nothing demonic about them. The same is true of instruments. How could one instrument be godly and another demonic? The person who plays the instrument should be the focus of our attention – are they godly, filled with the Holy Spirit? Neither, in worship, is style important. How could it be? God is primarily concerned about the state of the worshipper's heart. Style and form are not issues that He cares very much about at all. Personal preference and cultural distinctions are often used as an excuse to close down something we are afraid of. By saying a musical idiom is 'demonic' you are actually implying that the person playing the music is of the devil. Jesus rebuked Peter for using worldly wisdom, calling it satan (Mark 8:33). To paraphrase John Wimber, 'We put too much emphasis on satan's ability to deceive us and not enough on God's ability to lead us into new things.' What we really need is **balance**. My favorite definition of balance is 'the ability to embrace all valid extremes'. It is also very good physics too!

Music has an incredible power and I believe it has the ability to amplify the musician's spirit. It is a radical thought, but I believe that when a musician plays or sings, something is created that is amplifying that person's spirit. Do you remember the time Jesus went out on the water in a boat because He wanted to talk to the crowd of people on the shore? After He had gone a little way He stopped and turned around to address the crowd. The reason He did that was because the water had the power to amplify the sound of His voice – He used natural elements to amplify His voice to the crowd. Just as Jesus voice was amplified by the water, music can amplify the voice of God's Spirit within us.

Music itself has a spiritual quality to it because it originated in the Spirit and heart of God. God lives in it, God breathes through it. God is Spirit and music is a language of the spirit. There can be nothing demonic about 'a note' – all you are doing is moving some air. Music can only be thought of as demonically influenced if it is 'amplifying' the spirit of someone who is opposed to Christ. If music is being corrupted in this way, then it can be powerfully used as a negative force. Our enemy corrupts it all the time. But music in the hands of a believer, filled with the Spirit of God, is a wonderful and liberating thing. So often we throw out the baby with the bath water, to our loss. I believe we are experiencing the birth pains of another reformation in the Church, where music and art that slipped out the Church's grasp is being claimed back by God's people. All kinds of music is being reclaimed for use in worshipping God. It must happen! An important part of this journey will be helping the Church to be freed from such superstitions and Gnostic thought patterns.

A word for worship leaders

Although I want to strongly state that I believe all kinds of styles, forms and instruments are valid for use in our worship, and that as the Church, we need to take off the blinkers of personal preference, I would also sound a note of caution to worship leaders. One of the greatest assets a worship leader can have is sensitivity – to be sensitive, of course to the Holy Spirit, but also to the needs of the congregation. We have to face the reality (though we would dearly love to get past it) that there will be many shades of preference amongst the people. Your job is to lead them into God's presence, not to alienate them because of **your** personal preferences. All styles are valid, and personally I long to see more variety – the use of classical and also ethnic music. If we broaden our horizons and refuse to remain blinkered, we can grow and learn and progress together. We will experience increasing freedom in our worship to God. Creativity, music and art will truly be restored to the Church. My own personal pilgrimage has led me to believe that a vital component in this process is the relationship between church leader and worship leader. There must be a mutual recognition of gift and spiritual authority. When this happens people are released to be and do what they were meant to!

God wants to make each one of us into radical, passionate, obedient, worshipping followers of Christ. That is why He is taking so much trouble to call **you** as musicians, artists and creative people and equip you. Seek God today and ask Him to give you a revelation of the gifts you have and the part you will play in the end-time army that God is calling forth in the earth. Seek always to be a servant of the Body of Christ (and a pleasure to work with!).

Selah...

'Among the first things created was the bird. Why? Because God wanted the world to have music at the start. And this infant world, wrapped in swaddling clothes of light so beautifully serenaded at the start is to die amid the ringing blast of the archangel's trumpet; so that as the world had music at the start, it is going to have music at the last.'

(Thomas De Witt Talmage; 1832–1902)

Lord teach us how to pray, how to align ourselves with you and what you want to hear. Help us to hear heavenly sounds, to see heavenly colors and pictures and to speak heavenly words so that we might bring heaven down to earth. Lord we pray for new things, for higher things. Take us to higher places as we draw near to you. Help us to put our roots deep down and allow you to take us on to deeper things. Give us a strategy to go behind enemy lines and take back **everything** that has been stolen.

Notes

1. Westminster Larger Catechism. Full quote: *'Man's chief and highest end is to glorify God, and fully to enjoy him forever.'* Copyright EPC 1997.

2. John Chrysostom – an early Church Father, born in Antioch, Syria, circa AD 349–407. Exact date of birth is disputed.

3. See 1 Chronicles 12:32. The listing of David's army at Hebron includes, *'... the sons of Issachar who had understanding of the times, to know what Israel ought to do ...'*

Chapter 4

Discovering Your Destiny and Purpose

'For we are his workmanship, created in Christ Jesus for good works, which God prepared beforehand, that we should walk in them.'
(Ephesians 2:10)

In this chapter I want to talk about destiny and purpose, in my experience, a rarely taught concept in church. I am very grateful to Dr Myles Munroe of the Bahamas for helping me to unlock my thoughts in this area. God is about the business of restoring worship in spirit and truth to the Church. Part of the problem is that we as individuals have not realized the great potential that is latent within us. Through the work of Christ on the cross we were reconciled with God, and He is able to bring us into line with His predestined plan and purpose for our lives. All the gifts and abilities He gave us when we were born have their use in His purposes for us. True creativity will abound in the Church as God's people awake and realize who they are.

God is a God of order and purpose. He is a God of destiny. He has specific plans that He is working to, and is the master strategist. If you take time to consider the order that exists within His creation, you will see that everything holds together in a finely balanced tension. It should come as no surprise to us then to discover that, as the opening Ephesians scripture says, God has a specific plan for each of our lives. He has **good work** already planned for each one of us – work that is essential to the working of the overall plan. Here is a biblical paradox that has puzzled God's people throughout history: how can we be, at the same time, so inconsequential compared to God's awesome power and yet so vital to His methods and plans?

God's 'life plans' are not drawn up in isolation either, they are all seamlessly intertwined, one with another. Many people's lives and destinies are 'woven' together by God to outwork His plans. This is because God is a God of community and family. He desires each of us to serve His and one another's purposes in an emerging new kingdom. He has invested in His people the right to belong to a new nation, not like a nation of this world, but a nation whose habitation is a New Kingdom. We are all called to be members of the household of God.

Ephesians 2:19–22 tells us:

> ' ... *that we are no longer strangers and foreigners but fellow citizens with the saints and members of the household of God. Having been built on the foundations of all the apostles and prophets, Jesus Christ, himself being the chief corner-stone, in whom the whole building being fitted together, grows up into a holy temple in the Lord, in whom you are also being built together for a dwelling place of God in the spirit.'*

This passage shows us that in God's economy there is a place for every single person – regardless of social standing, race, ability, or any other number of different factors. God wants to inhabit a holy temple of praise and worship made from **all** His people joined together. As far as He is concerned the building is not fully complete if just one person is missing. This is the bigger picture that we must have in mind as we seek to connect with our God-given destiny. Finding your destiny is about realizing who you are in Christ, becoming confident in the knowledge of it, and then being prepared to become an 'anonymous' contributor to the greater purposes of God for His Church and the whole earth.

Some of the most important and fundamental questions that human beings ask themselves are, '**who am I?**' '**why am I here?**' and '**what is life all about ... is it possible to know?**' Every single person on this earth, regardless of how successful (or otherwise) they may be, will at some time have experienced that unquantifiable feeling that they have some-how missed the mark. That their life isn't quite what it should be, or that they were born for something different, something better than 'this'. This inevitably occurs when someone has failed to connect with their God-given purpose, perhaps because they do not know Christ, or have not yet received the revelation of their destiny as a Christian.

Why do we need to address this issue in this book? Because it is very, very important to know who you are. If you know who you are and what you have been called to do you will be a very dangerous person to the forces of darkness. People who don't really know who they are or what they are called to do, pose no threat to the enemy. It has been said, 'You cannot know **who** you are until you know **whose** you are'! You can then go on to work out **what** you are! The extent to which you are confident in your calling, and what God has called you to do, will be the extent to which you can take back what has been lost and stolen from you.

In 1976 Pink Floyd wrote on their *Dark Side of the Moon* album, 'hanging on in quiet desperation is the English way'. It has been said that most people live a life of quiet despera-tion. Silently going about their business while trying to live up to impossibly high standards. If today you are not walking in your true destiny and purpose in God, no matter what you do, you will always have that 'there has got to be more to life than this!' feeling. I happen to think that as Christians we are more susceptible to this problem than unbelievers. Some people have given up attributing any meaning to life! 'This is just the way it is ... this is as good as it gets,' is their rationalistic philosophy. Christians, however, are meant to know who they are and where they are going, aren't they?

However blessed we are during our worship times in our churches, and however fulfilled we are in our small groups, we may have to go through the rest of the week with a feeling of emptiness that we really don't like admitting to anybody else, because we are supposed to be 'Spirit-filled Christians'. We know that we're expected to be radiant with the glory of God but we're not and we don't like admitting it to anybody because it makes us feel guilty. The idea that as Christians we are never to have any problems, always laughing and triumphant, is a myth perpetuated by the enemy to keep Christians miserable – because we know that reality doesn't match up to this ideal! Jesus said,

> *'In this world you will have trouble. But take heart! I have overcome the world.'*   (John 16:33)

We have a misunderstanding of what glory really is. Paul said,

> *'We rejoice in the hope of the glory of God. Not only so, but we also rejoice in our sufferings, because we know that suffering produces perseverance; perseverance produces character; and character, hope.'*   (Romans 5:3)

Have you ever gone outside on a clear night and actually stood for a moment and looked up at the stars? What do you experience at that moment? Do you feel a sense of desperation or do you feel a sense of destiny? Do you feel that you are being called by God to do something but you're not quite sure what it is? Actually this feeling is more common than you might think. God has put eternity in men's hearts (Ecclesiastes 3:11) and for the redeemed it is more poignant because as Christians we have inherited a new identity and a new territory. We are living in the same world, but now viewing it from a completely different perspective. The way the Bible says it is that we are being transferred from one kingdom to another kingdom – from the kingdom of darkness into the kingdom of light (Colossians 1:12; Ephesians 5:8; see also 1 Peter 2:9; 1 Thessalonians 5:5). In this new kingdom it is possible to come into line with the destiny and purpose of God for our lives.

Many people think that the 'Born Again' experience is all there is to Christianity. You get born again and eventually go to heaven. Maybe they also discover about being filled with the Holy Spirit and say, 'OK, well this is the next thing. That's it, I've got it all, I'm in possession of it all now.' That's like going on holiday to a foreign country and spending all your time in passport control at the border! But this new territory, this kingdom of light, has new laws, new principles, new dynamics, and is far more expansive than we can dare to imagine.

If you think about it long enough and honestly enough, you will have to admit that it is possible to live as a born again, Spirit-filled Christian, and still carry with you a deep sense of un-fulfillment. You may have fasted, prayed, read the Bible and agonized over your future with God, and yet still not received clear answers to your questions, and still be wondering at the end of the day what it is all about. And yet Jesus clearly said,

> *'I have come, so that they may have life and have it in abundance.'*   (John 10:10)

'Abundance' means 'a lot' – a lot of life, a lot of fulfillment, a lot of purpose. Is this because God deliberately wants to make it hard for us to discover His purpose for us? I don't think so! Maybe it is because we are sometimes wanting Him to sanction things that we want to do, but that He knows won't do us any good. Or is it because we are sometimes very good at talking to God, but not so good at listening?

On one occasion back in 1980, I was sitting in a church when I heard the voice of the Holy Spirit talking to me very clearly. During the communion He said to me 'Open your eyes David.' At the time it was the norm to keep one's eyes shut whilst taking communion – everyone would close their eyes whilst praying, so that was quite radical for a start! But as I obeyed and looked around the church of about 500 people, a whole row of people seemed to turn into tombstones. A sense of deep sadness came upon me, and I sensed the Lord say to me, 'My people are living in death, they are not living in life. They are not living in the life that I came to buy for them. They have come to the foot of the cross, given their lives to Me, they've been filled with the Spirit, but that's where they've stopped. They have stayed there and not journeyed onward.' Jesus came to give abundant life and won a great victory at the cross. But He never intended us to stay there, expecting us to walk on into destiny and purpose. I believe that Christians have been fooled into accepting a lie. And the lie is this: being saved is the end of the matter, the ultimate purpose of life. But Scripture says it is only the beginning. It's not the Omega, it is the Alpha.

> *'For we are created in Christ Jesus for good works, which God prepared beforehand, that we should walk in them.'*
> (Ephesians 2:10)

Now if Jesus was a boring person and God was a miserable old father with no imagination at all, then our jobs – these works referred to in Ephesians 2:10 – would be very tedious. But as it is, Jesus is not boring, He is very exciting and God our Father is the greatest mind in the universe. Jesus was dynamic, energetic, exciting, enthusiastic, happy, fulfilled and passionate. He was an incredible person to be around. Jesus didn't say 'Well I suppose I'm just getting by doing the will of God.' He was the sort of person more likely to say, 'Wow, listen guys, this is what My Father is really like, you must meet Him!'

We are called by the Father with a purpose, with a destiny, and with a function in mind. Let me give you a very simple illustration. In my office at home I have a mug. This mug is filled with pens and pencils. Although it helps to keep me organized, I'm sure the manufacturer never envisaged it being used in such a way. Actually, I'm abusing its purpose. Myles Munroe would say that 'abuse' is literally 'ab-use' – abnormal use. There are hundreds of thousands of people in the world today walking around, ignorant of their purpose in Christ, trying to fill their lives with something that will make them look useful; wanted; needed.

If my coffee mug could speak, perhaps it would say 'Well I suppose I'm doing the will of God, I'm holding something, I mean I've been useful, I've got pens and pencils in me, I'm being a useful object in the House of God.' But if I actually took all the pens and pencils out and poured coffee into it, it would say 'Ah, now I understand what I was created for. I'm holding liquid!' When people discover their destiny and purpose in Christ, life takes on new meaning for them. Everything makes a great deal more sense.

In Genesis 1:26–28 God says, *'Let Us make man in Our image, according to Our likeness . . . '* God created man in His own image and then instructed him in verse 28, *'Be fruitful, and multiply; fill the earth and subdue it.'* God's purpose for man and woman was that they should represent Him on the earth, but things went badly wrong through their disobedience to Him. Communication with God the Father was finished and mankind progressively lost the knowledge of God's destiny for them.

By the time three or four generations had passed the paradise of Eden was almost completely forgotten. The name of one of Adam and Eve's grandsons literally meant 'Who is God?' Within a very short time man had lost his sense of destiny and purpose and mankind was doomed to stumble around, not knowing where they were going, because they didn't have the light of God to show them. Mankind has suffered from this curse ever since. No wonder we live in a world full of problems. Whole nations have lost their purpose, their destiny and their significance. When things lose their sense of purpose, the result is chaos – no order, just random elements doing their own thing.

We have established that God has a destiny and purpose planned out for each one of us; one that, as we begin to live in His kingdom, we will come increasingly into line with. But what about those who have so far failed to discover their purpose. What about those who are walking in the Spirit to the best of their knowledge and yet still feel unfulfilled? I hope that together with God, we can uncover some secrets that will help us.

Selah ...

'The creation of a thousand forests is in one acorn.'
(Ralph Waldo Emerson; 1803–1882)

Chapter 5

The Creator's Design

When individuals fail to discover their destiny and purpose, societies, communities, organizations, friendships, marriages, churches and nations are all affected. The result? Frustration, confusion, discouragement, disillusionment, anger, suicide, apathy, boredom, purposelessness, and lack of meaning. That's why some people drive themselves to succeed. They are looking for significance and to give meaning to their existence. That's why people find it threatening to be challenged sometimes about their life, their reason for living. People don't want to have to face up to questions like 'Is there any real meaning to life, or are we just all condemned by a cruel, unreachable God to live out our lives with a sense of desperation and frustration?' The prospect of it is too horrible for them to contemplate, so they'd rather not think about it at all.

In Ecclesiastes 1:2 Solomon wrote, *'Meaningless, Meaningless, all is meaningless.'* He had tried everything and the whole book of Ecclesiastes is about his increasingly frustrated search for purpose, destiny and meaning. It's the natural cry of a heart without God, and nothing has changed in human nature since his day. There is much motion, a lot of activity, but little purpose, no vision and no passion. 'Ceaseless but unproductive activity' A.W. Tozer called it. Many have realized this, and not knowing the answer have opted to 'get out'. They have withdrawn from society to live like recluses.

If meaninglessness is the result of not knowing one's purpose, then what is the result of knowing one's purpose? Solomon in all his glory and wisdom, didn't know what we, the Church know. It's been right under our noses for years. We can't have grasped Jesus' words and held on to them, because He clearly said,

> *'I have come that they may have life and have it more abundantly.'*   (John 10:10)

Only through Jesus' death and resurrection can we find our destiny and purpose with any degree of certainty at all. The first key to anyone finding their purpose must be to find Christ.

The result of walking in one's purpose and destiny is strength, clarity of direction, fulfillment, satisfaction and focus. One of the reason's why I can often be very determined and persistently strong, is because I know who I am. We can find out what our purpose is because through Christ the veil that prevented our having an intimate personal knowledge of God, has been torn down the middle. We can go into the Holy of Holies and say,

> 'Father, please will you show me what are my good works that You have designed for me? I'm asking because I don't want to try to do someone else's work, I want to do the work for which you have designed me. I want to be able to say "Eureka, I've found it!"'

Another key to finding your purpose – and I'm thinking now about those who have found Christ and so have been redeemed into God's plan – is design. Think again about that mug in my office, holding my pens, but actually designed to hold liquid. When it receives liquid, it is being subjected to normal use. Clues to use can be found in the way that something has been designed. You wouldn't design something to hold liquid and put a hole in the bottom of it! You would design it not to leak because its very purpose is to hold liquid. God has given you and me certain natural gifts and abilities. He has designed us to function in a certain way. In Christ those gifts and abilities can find their ultimate fulfillment. We should not be surprised that God wants to use those natural talents we have in a redemptive way.

I saw this most clearly many years ago, while still puzzling over the Genesis account of creation. Because of the humanistic values I had been taught at school, masquerading as 'science', I grew up believing in an evolutionary philosophy that ruled out the possibility of a 'Creator'. At that time, my daughter was quite small and I had taken her one Sunday afternoon, for a visit to the Natural Science and History Museum in London.

I had been explaining to her basic truths from the Bible and came face to face with a large display. It consisted of a row of cabinets and in them were certain bones that had been taken from different animals. There were obvious similarities in the way these animals had been constructed. Inside were the bones of small rodents and birds and the display was intended to prove that an evolutionary process had taken place between them. They were in essence saying that the incredible wealth of creativity shown forth in creation was nothing more than a series of providential cosmic developments.

I wondered how I should explain this to my little daughter and as I prayed about it, God spoke to me and I suddenly realized that the similarity in the bones was not because there had been a development from one to the other. The similarities in construction were there because they were designed to perform the same type of function in each of the different creatures.

It makes sense that when you arrive at a perfect design for something, you simply use that pattern and adapt it for various applications. God the Father came up with the perfect design and He used it for everything; they were similar because they had been designed by the same mind. The design that God has decided on for something is a clue to its purpose.

Once someone has heard from God and connected with their true destiny and purpose, no amount of persuasion would pull them away from it. You could offer them a million dollars to do something different, but they would say, 'No thank you, because I've found my destiny, I've found my purpose and God's Plan-A for my life.' My 'redeemed' mug would never be satisfied again with holding pens for me! This is where we all need to get to.

You need to know who you are and what God has called you to do. What is **your** good work? Because if you are confident in the purpose for your existence, you will be fulfilled. You will find your destiny and it will produce motivation, commitment, hope, passion and vision for your life. Complacency will fade and you will have a reason for getting up in the morning. Your vision and call will hold you through the tough times and give meaning and purpose to your life. Now that sounds more like fullness of life to me!

You are a one-off, a unique person. There is no-one on the face of the earth who is like you! You are not a copy or an echo; you are an original. People who fail to realize this often try to copy someone else. They try to be other people. They mistakenly think that 'If it works for so-and-so, then it will work for me.' As artists they may tend to adopt methods that have been successful for others. Essentially there's nothing wrong with that as a means of learning. God's providence is certainly big enough to allow us to learn, make mistakes, and perhaps copy what others are doing for a while. He says that's OK for a time. But ultimately He has put you on this earth because you are a unique expression of His love. Nobody can express God quite like you, and so your fulfillment in life depends on your becoming and doing what you were born to be and do! This is the first principle of the new kingdom you've been called to live in: you must pursue finding your destiny and purpose with all of your heart.

Allow me to finish by giving you a few more clues to connecting with your God-given purpose. Certain things that have happened to me have greatly helped me to realize who I was. Perhaps you, like me, have been thinking about this for a long time. Almost as soon as I became a Christian, my cry was 'God, what do you want me to do?' I've been a Christian since 1979 and I've been thinking about it ever since. A real turning point for me was when God spoke to me through the book of Isaiah,

> 'Fear not, for I have redeemed you; **I have called you by your name**, you are mine.'   (Isaiah 43:1)

The fact that God calls you **by name** is significant. Often people's names say something about who they are and what they are meant to do.

I have three daughters and when my first daughter was born, we weren't Christians. She's 33 years old now and her name is Sarah. When she was born, my wife and I decided that her name was going to be Rachel. I walked into the hospital and saw this little girl and I thought 'That's not a Rachel, that's a Sarah!' (meaning **princess**), and so when I went to register the baby, I registered her as Sarah. My wife was very cross with me, because I didn't tell her! However, she forgave me and then later on we had another daughter. Before she was born we had thought of calling her Emma. But again, when I first laid eyes on her I thought 'She's not an Emma, she's an Alison' (meaning **truthful**). Again when it came time to register the baby, I registered her as Alison, and again my wife wasn't very pleased with me!

Eventually we had a late child, by which time we had become Christians, so this time we **prayed** about what her name should be, the Lord said, 'Call the baby Jessica.' When I saw her I thought, 'That's a Jessica' (meaning **God sees**, or **wealthy one**. As she's only 14, I'll have to wait and see whether or not the latter will enable her to look after her Dad in his old age!). All the girls' personalities accurately reflect the meaning of their names, and I believe the Lord gave me the names of all our children. I believe the Lord Himself also desires to give us names appropriate to the purpose for which He designed us.

The Jewish people believed in this strongly. They called the child a name that expressed what they saw in the child and what the child was to do. The names they gave to their children would usually have two aspects to them:

1. What they saw in the child – his or her natural attributes.
2. What they believed the child's destiny and purpose to be – his or her prophetic name.

My name, David, means 'Beloved'. My second name, Leonard, means 'Lionheart'. My surname, in England, could mean 'A Big Tent' or 'Covering', and in America, is a sign outside a cinema to say what's coming next. So, if you can accept that a tent is a tabernacle or a dwelling, and a sign bears witness to something, then my name could be, '**Beloved-Lionheart-Tabernacle**' or '**Beloved-Lionheart-Witness**.'

If you make a study of your name it may provide an important clue to your destiny in God. However, having received some revelation from God on this, don't be surprised if you think, 'I couldn't be more different from the name God has given me.' Your destiny and calling will always be resisted. The enemy is committed to trying to rob you of God's purposes for your life. I have had a tremendous battle in my life to arrive at knowing who I am and what I was destined to do. I was abused as a child and betrayed by my father while I was still at school. I come from a broken home. I was unjustly expelled from school when I was 14. I was bullied by a teacher at school.

If I am '**Beloved**' – how can I feel loved with all of that in my past? The enemy has done everything he can to come against that prophetic name of God over me and tried to destroy it. There have been many times when I have felt anything but 'beloved'.

If I am '**Lionheart**' – well, lions are known for their bravery and courage. Guess what I've had trouble with in life! Insecurity, fear, inferiority – everything that could possibly undermine the lionhearted element of my nature, the warrior part of me.

My last name – '**Tabernacle, Dwelling Place, a House of God**' – I believe, speaks of what God has called me to do: to help in restoring God's tabernacle. Music will play a great part in that.

The enemy has literally tried to kill me three times, just to stop that prophetic name achieving the purpose that God has decided upon. But when you know what your name is, you will also begin to understand where the enemy will try to attack you.

Patiently seeking God for the revelation of your destiny and purpose in Him is probably the single most important key that will open the door to your fulfillment. Going to Him in as childlike a way as possible, is a vital part of the process. When we seek God just because He is God, amazing things happen.

Having an open heart toward God, a willingness to listen for His voice, and the determination to seek His face until you meet with Him, are qualities that you will need to nurture if you are going to be successful in discovering your destiny in Him. When we come to God as children with no agenda, we find that He meets us just because He longs to spend time with us. We begin to discover our purpose as we discover more of Him. Steve Brown, professor of practical theology at the Reformed Seminary in Orlando, Florida, describes the experience this way:

> '...I prayed. Not the cold, formal prayer of the liturgy, but the prayer of a child in pain reaching out to a father. It was the cry of my soul for intimacy with the God of my life. I didn't bargain, I didn't pretend (I did enough of that with people), I didn't come with preconceived ideas of what God would do, and I didn't make demands. I simply came and asked to know Him ... God didn't come when I demanded it, but He came ... I encountered the God who is really there.'

When you encounter the living God you will discover the purpose He has for you, because the closer we get to Him, the more sense everything else makes.

Selah...

' "For I alone know the plans I have for you," declares the Lord, "Plans to prosper you and not to harm you, plans to give you hope and a future. Then you will call upon me and come and pray to me, and I will listen to you. You will seek me and find me when you seek me with all you heart. I will be found by you." '
                                    (Jeremiah 29:11–14a)

'All heaven is waiting to help those who will discover the will of God and do it.'   (J. Robert Ashcroft; 1878–1958)

Chapter 6

The Two Songs

The song of salvation

I love to hear great secular musicians and artists. I think they are wonderful, and I believe that many of them have an anointing from the Lord. That may shock some readers and I want to assure you that I do not use that word 'anointing' lightly. I believe that many talented artists we could name have a common grace that, through a life transformed by the power of Christ, would manifest itself as an even more holy and wonderful gift from God. Whether the person who has the gift knows Jesus right now or not, that gift is still God-given, still precious and with the potential to be wonderfully anointed. I have worked with people in my life who could play just one note and have an audience of three thousand people rising to their feet. Many classical concerts are powerful enough to elicit incredible reactions. All of us have heard music, seen paintings, read literature and gone to movies that have thrilled us, because even though we know non-believers created them, we have sensed God in them – something in our spirits recognized His divine fingerprints on the work.

One of the things that I have discovered is that music is a creative gift, given by God. Like any other art-form, it is creative, but it is not redemptive. I have made a case already for believing that the angels, who sang at the dawn of creation, probably fell down with Lucifer who became satan. However, these angels are only able to sing one song – the song of creation. This is what they were doing at the beginning of the universe (Job 38:4–7).

The Bible says the wonder and **mystery** of salvation through the grace of God that has been revealed to us, is something that the angels long to look into (1 Peter 1:12). God's grace is a source of inspiration to us that the angels cannot fathom. Musicians and artists who have experienced the miracle of salvation are naturally more in touch with the spiritual aspects of life than non-believers. The Holy Spirit that God has put within those who are born again, is the same Person who was involved with the creation of the universe. He alone is the source of creative power, and those who are His should always be reaching out, always pioneering, always discovering, always creating new things.

There is much great music to be heard in the world. Nevertheless, beautiful music from great and gifted composers, is still only a song of creation. I can point to many wonderfully gifted musicians and singers who only sing one song – the song of creation, and the world applauds it.

In the mid 1980s, a pastor called James Ryle got into a lot of trouble because he said something that many felt was an outrageous statement. He said that the Beatles were anointed and their music was anointed by God. He took a real hammering for making that statement. But I believe he was right. The Bible tells us that God pours His spirit out on **all** flesh. He doesn't say 'I will pour My Spirit out on Christian flesh,' He says *'I will pour My Spirit out on all flesh'* and that included the Beatles. There is a strong case for it biblically. The song of creation **is** anointed. The Beatles were manifesting a creativity that was prophetic, but it was without redemption because they didn't know the Creator. ✗

Just like Martin Luther, the Wesley brothers and William Booth did with the popular songs of their day, I have sometimes sung Beatles songs and changed the lyrics to Christian ones! Songs like *She Loves You* with the chorus changed to 'He Loves you' with a few minor word changes, can become powerful prophetic statements to the Church, as if the Father Himself were singing it over His children. If *'He rejoices over us with singing'* (Zephaniah 3:17), I wonder what He sings?

As Christians, we have a huge advantage over other gifted, and yet spiritually blind people. The book of Revelation talks about another song. This is the song that the elders and the

✗ Rom. 11:29 KJV

redeemed all sing in heaven before the throne of God – the **song of salvation**. No one can sing this song unless they have an intimate knowledge of the Lord Jesus Christ. People on earth may do incredible things with instruments, wonderful things with theatre, paint beautiful pictures, write poignant books and make inspiring movies, but without Jesus they all miss the point, and missing the target either by one milli-metre or one metre is still missing! The point is that the Lord Jesus Christ came two thousand years ago, hung on a cross and bought back everything that we had lost. Most import-antly He gave us a redeemed relationship with the Father through the forgiveness of sins, but He also redeemed for us the most beautiful things – love songs and stories that all have the themes of redemption and salvation in them. All the best movies that touch our hearts have the theme of redemp-tion or salvation in them. The courage of the hero laying his life down to rescue somebody in trouble; the orphan finding a family; the useless finding purpose. The best songs, movies and art always reflect the theme of redemption, because they reflect hope for humanity.

The song of creation is still echoing all around the world, very much in evidence. An almost prophetic, creative voice coming from people who don't know Jesus. It bears the fingerprints of God and it touches our spirits, mirroring God's own creativity, and trying to mirror His image.

Psalm 150 is a famous passage of Scripture I'm sure you'll have heard quoted many times. Verse 6 says, *'Let everything that has breath praise the Lord.'* **Everything!** This scripture and many others point to the fact that there will come a day when the whole of creation will bow the knee and praise the Lord – either willingly or forcibly. Bob Dylan said, 'You gotta serve somebody ... it may be the devil or it may be the Lord, but you gotta serve somebody!' [1] As Christians we are the only ones who can sing the song of salvation because we know the Saviour.

Psalm 150 makes mention of drums and cymbals. The drums are powerfully prophetic. Perhaps that's one of the reasons why they have been so maligned in the Church. In the African country of Burundi drummers often form an essential part of church services. They have several rows of them, sometimes 20 or 30 drummers all playing at once. They praise God with their drums and you can feel the anointing, it is absolutely incredible.

God loves to hear you!

There has been so much misunderstanding in the Church over the years that I want to repeat my earlier statement: **Music is from the Spirit**. Our creativity is a reflection of God and when we use those gifts to His glory, He loves it. He is very, very happy. You make Him happy when you play, sing, and when you use your gift.

If you gave a little child a present and he said thank you, but then never unwrapped it, you would think it strange. If the child took it away and put it on a shelf, going from time to time to look at it, what would you think? If it was an expensive present and you had spent a lot of money on it, you would think 'I wish I hadn't bothered. All it's doing is gathering dust on the shelf.'

God absolutely loves it when you use what He has given you; it's almost like we can feel His pleasure. God **is** creativity. God gave creativity away to us because He is a giving God – the kind of God that like to give things away. He made sure that man was created 'in His image' with creative ability.

Lucifer (when he had the ability to dwell in God's presence), was told to cover God's throne with praises and fill the air with praise and singing. He had to 'fill up' the airwaves, the whole spectrum. His job was to magnify God. Because he became proud and was cast down, that privilege now rests with us. God loves to be enthroned on the praises of His people. While we are magnifying God with our praise and worship, the presence of God is enhanced in a wonderful way. It's amazing that a human has been given the ability to do that. My own particular gift as a musician is what I call a 'Romans Gift', a natural gifting; a common grace gift, such as James Ryle observed that the Beatles had. I am not the only bass player, there are far greater players than me, but some of them don't know Jesus.

The praise of God and living in God's presence actually beautifies a person. Worshipping God and spending time with Him is the most effective beauty treatment you could ever have! People glow when they have been in the presence of God, they shine (Exodus 34:30; Acts 6:15). There is such a relaxation in God's presence. If you spend at least as much time in the presence of God as you do in the bathroom, it will certainly benefit you!

Selah...

'Whatever is true, whatever is worthy of reverence and is honorable and seemly, whatever is just, whatever is pure, whatever is lovely and loveable, whatever is kind and winsome and gracious, if there is any virtue and excellence, if there is anything worthy of praise, think on these things fix your mind on them.' (Philippians 4:8 Amplified Bible)

Note

1. Dylan, Bob, 'Gotta Serve Somebody', from the album *Slow Train Coming*, (Columbia, 1979).

Chapter 7

The Song God Longs to Hear

Isaiah 55:12 says:

> *'For you shall go out with joy, and be led out with peace; The mountains and the hills shall break forth into singing before you, and all the trees of the field shall clap their hands.'*

Even the mountains and hills are depicted as breaking into song in this passage. Why? Because creation sings. It is so impregnated with the glory of God that it cannot help but bear witness to His goodness. But even though all creation sings, God is longing for the song of salvation to ring out across the earth. There is redemption in this song, not just creation, and it exalts His beloved Son, Jesus Christ.

Isaiah 44:23 says:

> *'Sing, O heavens, for the Lord has done it! Shout, you lower parts of the earth; break forth into singing you mountains, O forest, and every tree in it! For the Lord has redeemed Jacob, and glorified Himself in Israel.'*

This is an incredible line. Because He has redeemed Jacob, the Lord is overjoyed. God is talking about displaying His glory in the earth. This is the central idea of our teaching here. If you forget everything else that is written in this book, remember this: it is only the God of Glory who will fully satisfy you. That urging within your heart is the fundamental desire to use your gift to worship and glorify God. So go for the true gold – the glory of God.

The first rebels in the universe were angelic beings who rebelled in heaven. They were originally designed to give praise to God, but they are far from fulfilling that call now.

Our own abilities and gifts are a natural part of our design too. That doesn't mean they won't function at all without God, but if they do they will lack the elements of redemption and salvation. Please don't misunderstand me here. I am not saying that every single song you write should contain John 3:16 somewhere. That has been another hang-up of the Church. But we have a special relationship with Jesus that facilitates a growing love for Him. We have a unique capacity to reflect the Father, and our gifts will function at their best when they are being surrendered to the Holy Spirit and allowed to become tools He can use.

God decided to embrace man in a way He never has with the angels. Man has a unique capability to be in a relationship with Him. Mankind sits with the Father in Glory. There is a man in heaven **now**. His name is Jesus. Jesus didn't go back to being anything else. He became a man for us, and as a man He went back to sit with the Father.

Because of our unique relationship with God, through Christ, we have now taken over Lucifer's old job. We are now the worship leaders. Lucifer hates it when the Church discovers and really takes hold of the fact that we now have the authority to cover the Throne of God with praise and to guard the presence of God. God threw the worship leader out and started again with mankind. It is our responsibility. As you read these words, I pray that you will be filled with a new confidence, that you have been given the capacity to fill the airwaves with praise. Use your imagination to creatively worship and magnify the Lord! It used to be Lucifer's job, but now it is **yours**! This is why there is a battle taking place.

Ephesians 2:6, 7 says:

> *'God raised us up in Christ and seated us with him in the heavenly realms in Christ Jesus, in order that in the coming ages he might show forth the incomparable riches of his grace expressed in his kindness to us in Christ Jesus.'*

I want you to realize what a position you are in! Seated with Christ in heaven! Whether you feel ready for that, or worthy enough, is not important. God has chosen to lavish His grace on you.

Sin results in separation from God and redemption leads to reconciliation. We are called to be agents of reconciliation. God is a relational God. His angels are ministering servants, but they are not sons and daughters, and God desires children not servants. It's very important we understand that God is calling us to be sons and daughters. A servant does not need a relationship with his master; he just does what he is told. But sons and daughters have a unique place of privilege within their father's household. You will begin to minister much more effectively when you begin to realize just who you are! You are children of the King and the focus of His love. The revelation of this truth makes serving Him a joy, not a duty.

Some years ago I had the privilege of praying with Larry Norman. He was mightily used by God in a very prophetic way in the early 1960s Jesus Movement. He was probably the father of Christian rock music and knew that God had called him to be a servant. He came to our town and became a friend of mine and God gave me a message for him. I went to his concert and said I had a word for him from the Lord. God wanted me to tell him that He was his Father and he didn't have to be a servant. He said to me later that he had told God he wouldn't believe anybody unless they could tell him something that only he knew. He had been struggling for years with this concept of servanthood and son-ship. We ministered to him and he says it transformed his ministry, because now he was not doing it out of a sense of duty, or admiration, or even the knowledge that Christ was the answer. He was now ministering out of love for his Father. He was saying the same things and singing the same songs, but the spirit that was now coming through it was the spirit of sonship, not servanthood, and as such it was appealing directly to the heart. If you can reach somebody's heart, you can capture all of the person, and once you have someone on a heart level they bring their minds with them.

The worshipper's heart

It is the heart of a person that is all-important to God. That is why He took such a lot of trouble with David and why David is such an important biblical figure – because of his heart. David's heart was open before God, and God loved his heart. Even though he lived the same kind of life as you and I, making both good decisions and bad, God blessed his line because He loved David's heart. David loved God with a passion and was always able to go back to his Father even when he made bad mistakes. He loved God's people, and he loved the creativity of God. The history of music would be incomplete without some mention of David, because music played such a large part in his ministry. Apart from being a fantastic administrator, a warrior and a great general he was a king and a priest. He was also a gifted psalmist and musician. David even invented instruments and he must have been the sort of guy who heard a sound in his spirit and thought, 'There is no instrument here which can give me that sound, so I'll make one.'

The wonderful thing about David was that he knew God's anointing and he also knew God's great forgiveness. But he was a person that many would have thrown out of church! Not only did he have an affair with one of his general's wives, he arranged that the general would get killed in battle, and then he had an illegitimate baby with her. We would have thrown him out, but God used David to bring the Messiah's line. Jesus was born from David's family. It is an incredible testament to God's forgiveness and restoration. David knew what it was like to be a sinner and the Bible says that he who is forgiven much, loves much. If you have been forgiven something really big and you know forgiveness yourself, you can't help forgiving others.

True worship is tied to this sort of thankfulness. One of the major themes of worship is to come before the Lord with thanksgiving. When we enter into God's presence, even if we are having a hard time in our lives, at least there is one thing we can thank Him for which will never go away – for saving us and forgiving us. So at times when you feel a little down, just remember how much you have been forgiven, and as you thank Him for that loudly and say 'Thank you Lord for my salvation, for the cross, for saving me,' you can begin to enter the courts of praise.

Angels don't know forgiveness because they don't need to

be saved, but we do. That allows us to sing this song. The enemy would like to take away your birthright, the right you have to function in your God-given destiny and purpose, doing the work that God has asked you to do. God desires to be enthroned on the praises of His people. The whole earth must rise up in praise, worship and adoration of the Creator. This is what creation itself is waiting for, and we must play our part in it.

The battle for the airwaves

We are living in an age where the battle to dominate the airwaves is intensifying. The information already occupying the airwaves right now through the Internet, TV and radio is incredible. We live in an age of information, and Lucifer is trying to fill the airwaves with his propaganda – things that will distract people away from God. I believe that God is calling a company of people not only to work in the Church, covering the throne of God with praise, but also to take that praise to the gates of the city – into the media, into concert halls; to fill the air with godly praise; to fill art galleries and books, and to dance. I believe that we are called to be a part of this end-time army. It is an expression of appreciation to God, an expression of entering into the Lord's gates – the gates of His presence – with thanksgiving.

God is raising up generals in every strata of society right now. There are certain people I know of that God is raising up in the media. He seems to be repositioning people and exalting certain ones to positions of influence, raising up people who have a heart that is thankful. They know they have been forgiven, they know they have been set free and they have worked it out to a point where God can trust them because He knows their heart is like David's heart. He knows that even if they fall they will go back to Him.

Let me remind you of the scripture in Ephesians:

> 'Therefore you are no longer strangers and foreigners, but
> fellow citizens with the saints and members of the household
> of God having been built already on the foundation of
> the apostles and prophets, with Jesus Christ himself being

> *the chief cornerstone, in whom the whole building, being*
> *fitted together, grows up into a holy temple in the Lord.'*
> (Ephesians 2:19–22)

This is what God is doing. This is why God wants each of us to reach his or her potential. God wants a house. Where does He live? In the praises of His people. Where does praise start? In the heart, with thankfulness and gratefulness to the Lord as sons and daughters. No longer servants, but sons and daughters who are getting to know the Father and saying 'Father, show me your love that I may get to know you more and understand your greatness and kindness – that I may truly be your child.' This is thankfulness, and this is true worship.

Selah...

'There is no need to plead that the love of God shall fill our heart as though He were unwilling to fill us. He is willing as light is willing to flood a room that is opened to its brightness; willing as water is to flow into an emptied channel. Love is pressing round us on all sides like air. Cease to resist, and instantly love takes possession.' (Amy Carmichael; 1867–1951)

Chapter 8

Letting Go

Who's in control?

Although the Western Church has fallen behind the Church in countries such as Chile and Argentina, in terms of the outpouring of God's Spirit in renewal and revival, in the last five years or so many have experienced God in radical new ways. Without exception, as the Holy Spirit has touched people's lives in a dramatic way, He has sought to deal with issues of control in their lives. It is notable that the Holy Spirit pinpoints 'control' as one of the fundamental stumbling-blocks that prevents God's people from experiencing real intimacy with Him. We love to be in control. It makes us feel safe; in charge; masters of our own destiny – which of course we're not, or at least cannot afford to be if we are going to experience all that God has for us. Let me ask the question about your life: 'Who is in control? Who is in charge? Is it God, or is it you?'

Of course God is in charge ultimately, but He is not a controller, nor is He a manipulator. But, if the Lord knows there is a serious control issue in someone's life, He has to deal with it before that person can come to full maturity in Christ. He graciously shows us that unless we let go of the circumstances of our life, He can't take full control and bless us as He longs to. This is equally true of our tendency to control the use of our gifts and the way we try to control and manipulate others.

One of the main reasons why some people are afraid of revival and renewal is because they are afraid of not being in control any more. God is determined to get that independent, self-sufficient spirit out of us, and when He begins to work in great power, it can get pretty uncomfortable. I thank God that He gave us laughter while He was working on us, because that somehow softened the blow.

Allow me to share with you something of my own experience of the hand of God. I was working in a studio in Canada with my friend Dan Cutrona sometime around December 1993, just before God's Spirit fell on the Airport Vineyard Church in Toronto in January 1994. As we began our studio session, God visited us. His presence descended right into that studio. We were there to record an album and during a coffee break I picked up a guitar and started to worship the Lord. The presence of God came into the place so thick and so heavy, we ended up not recording a single note for the rest of the day! We couldn't because we didn't want to play, we just wanted to enjoy the Lord's presence.

I returned to England and around the end of February I got a phone call from Dan. 'I want you to come over to see what's going on in this church near the airport,' he said. 'I don't know if this is God or not; I can't tell. There's crazy things going on. People are shaking and laughing and crying and falling over, and running around the place, crying out to God and acting as if they are totally drunk.'

I finally got on an airplane to Toronto in the middle of May 1994 to see what was happening for myself. On the flight over I remember thinking to myself, 'If God has visited this place with so much of the power of His presence, then there are a few things I want to talk to Him about.' I got a 'shopping list' together, and I wanted to get answers to a whole list of different things. I walked into that church on a Sunday morning. It wasn't a huge place, but there were about a 1,000 people there, all jammed together, and when it came to the prayer time, some of them were doing some very strange things. It wasn't too long before I heard the voice of God speak to me and He said, 'Do you believe this is me?' It was as simple as that.

'David, do you believe this is Me?'

'Yes Lord,' I replied. 'I recognize Your Spirit, I know You're here.'

And He said to me 'Well, what are you going to do about it then?'

Well, my shopping list just went out the window and I just said 'Lord, whatever You want!' I just gave Him total control. I surrendered my life to Him again. I said to the Lord, 'Jesus, I'm going to trust You even more, You can do what You like.' That was the beginning of an incredible healing in my life.

God shows up back home

The most interesting thing however, happened when I got back home. I flew home from Toronto not as a musician, but as a pastor. I went into the office and it was the first time I had seen my staff since I had been away. My office manager, John Coburn, was at his desk and two other girls were working away. I have always disliked pettiness and small fiddly details, and John was a financial man who would write everything down. He came to me with a little plastic packet and in it was some coins that amounted to £1.21. He wanted me to sign a receipt.

I had just been in the presence of God for an incredible week. I had been on a mountain top with the God who owns the universe, and here was my financial manager standing with me saying 'Just sign this.' I was looking at him and all sorts of things were going around in my mind. I was thinking 'How am I going to get this blessing that I've just experienced back into the church? How is God going to come in great power, breaking out into revival? How many people are going to get saved and filled with the Holy Spirit? How many marriages are going to be put back together?' – and my financial manager wants me to sign a receipt for £1.21!

I felt this anger rise up inside of me and I was just about to say something to him. Actually, I wanted to be really sarcastic to him. I wanted to ask him, 'How many people is this going to save?' But before I could get anything out of my mouth, I felt the Holy Spirit push me in the back. I literally felt a hand in my back push me and very slowly I started to fall over. I fell over my chair and I ended up with my head in the waste paper basket! At that moment, my manager looked like a very small animal, caught in headlights! Eventually, I was lying under the desk and I could hear this knocking. 'What's that?' I thought, and as I looked, I saw that the Holy Spirit had got hold of John and he was bouncing up and down on the floor. I started laughing and he started laughing, then the other two girls in the office started laughing as well. We all laughed hysterically for about 20 minutes.

I decided then that it would be a good idea to get up and go to the bathroom. That was through the door and across the corridor. I managed to make it to the bathroom and by this time, both girls were on the floor and John, who was still shaking, had flipped over on his back and was lying under his desk amongst a maze of wires and computer bits, still laughing. And as I was coming out of the bathroom, the Holy Spirit hit me again and I ended up, lying flat on my back in the hallway, with one arm in the office door and my leg up the staircase, still laughing.

At that very moment, one of my leaders came in the front door. This man had come from a very formal church background and he stepped through the door to find his pastor absolutely 'out of it'. He had come to bring the Sunday offering in and he actually stepped over me and went into the office only to find more chaos. There were the two girls wrapped around each other somewhere in the corner of the office and my office manager, flapping like a fish on the floor. My leader told me later that he was quite offended by it, but I was not in control of that situation, God was! This leader had a hard time relating to what was happening because he also had control issues in his life that God desired to deal with.

Trusting that God is in charge

I want to emphasis again that the Holy Spirit wants to deal with these issues of control in your life. If you are longing for your gifts to be released and used by God in a mighty way, this will happen only through submission to Him. Surrender equals release. A person only wants to control the things that they cannot trust God for, or are just too afraid to let go of. We've got to decide who's in charge of our lives. The Bible teaches us the principle of the surrendered heart, humility, grace and submission. The more confident we become in trusting our heavenly Father, the less we have to try to control our circumstances. The extent to which we are trusting Him, is the extent to which we are able to let go.

Control versus biblical authority

A leader once approached me to talk through some problems he was having at his church. His musicians weren't turning up for practices or teaching sessions when they were supposed to, and didn't seem to recognize his leadership as they once did. He felt that the answer was for him to exercise greater authority over the musicians, thinking it would give him the 'control' he was lacking.

I said to him 'But you already have all the authority you need because you are the leader and everybody knows that. You don't need to remind them. Your authority is delegated anyway – it comes from God and He delegates it to you, so what's the problem?' The point is, he didn't need any more authority or control. He had already been given all the authority he needed to do his job. What he needed was to let go and allow God to step in.

Menno Simons, one of the founding fathers of the Mennonite Church, expressed this principle well when he said,

> 'Spiritual authority is never to make the rebel conform; its only purpose is to enable the obedient person to live a holy life. Therefore it rests on submission and obedience freely given. Furthermore, spiritual authority has only spiritual means at its disposal; its only weapons are prayer, scripture, counsel and the power of a holy life.' [1]

Further, let's look at what the Bible says about a leader's authority. Timothy said that if a man cannot rule his own household well, how can he rule God's house properly? (1 Timothy 3:1–13). The fact is that even a man's own children or his family can disqualify him from holding office in the Church. If somebody's children are disobedient and just do their own thing, then it points to the fact that they have not been brought up to respect proper authority. The Bible says that what a man sows he will reap. If he cannot exercise a loving, firm rule in his own house, then he will not be able to exercise a loving, firm leadership in God's house. The church members will not take any more notice of him then his own household do, and God will not allow any double standards in the Body of Christ. Many pastors and leaders have had to work through this difficult problem in their own lives.

If you find yourself in this position in your ministry, my advice would be to go before God and ask Him why those you are leading are not doing what you ask. We need to learn that authority in ministry comes from character, and to develop character takes time and hard work. It begins when we decide to humble ourselves before God and admit that we are powerless to make it work by ourselves.

Smith Wigglesworth once said,

> 'Your inner man needs to be as strong, if not stronger than, the gift and anointing God has given you to carry on His ministry in the earth.'

Character balanced with gift is vital. I'm not hasty to lay hands on anybody because I believe that sometimes, pastors are intimidated by a person's great gift and lay hands on them too quickly – they delegate authority to them before their character has been molded enough to accept it. Jesus talked a lot about what we call the 'little-much principle' – in other words, you start off with a little and prove yourself faithful with it, then you prove yourself faithful in greater and greater measure. God will only give you the authority that only He knows you can handle. I think that particularly in these days, God is after a people who won't walk with a double standard. If you want God to show up when you are called on to minister, then you need to make sure that your lifestyle is attracting the Lord to come and live at your house, or in your hotel room, or work place. He wants to be with you there just as much as He does in church. Let us seek to live with no double standards and we will experience true authority from God. God is no fool. He knows our hearts and He is a very forgiving, very loving Father, but He is absolutely committed to raising up an army of end-time, worship warriors.

Selah ...

'Because he has set his love upon Me, therefore will I deliver him; I will set him on high, because he knows and understands My name (has a personal knowledge of My mercy, love and kindness – trusts and relies on Me, knowing I will never forsake him, no, never). He shall call upon Me, and I will answer him; I will be with him in trouble, I will deliver him and honor him. With long life I will satisfy him and show him My salvation.'

(Psalm 91:14–16 Amplified)

'If we take God's program we can have God's power – not otherwise.' (E. Stanley Jones; 1884–1973)

Note

1. As quoted in *Understanding Leadership* by Tom Marshall, Sovereign World, 1991.

Chapter 9

Healing the Heart

Where can I go for help?

My major concern for artists, musicians and creative people
is that they be made whole – that they become whole
people in Christ. Years of misunderstanding and misuse at
the hands of the world, and sadly also the Church, has left a
great many hurting people. A lack of understanding about
the burden that is uniquely theirs to bear has left many more
broken at the side of the road. A great deal of healing needs
to take place, and although it won't happen overnight,
somebody has got to start somewhere. Our gifts can function
at their best when our characters are well-defined, balanced
and mature, and as long as we are wounded and hurting our
characters are suffering the consequences. Floyd McClung, in
his book *The Father Heart of God*, says,

> 'Emotional healing is almost always a process. It takes
> time. There is a very important reason for this. Our
> heavenly Father is not only wanting to free us from the
> pain of past wounds, He is also desirous of bringing us
> into maturity, both spiritually and emotionally. That
> takes time ... He loves us enough to take the months
> and years necessary to not only heal our wounds, but
> also build our character. Without growth of character
> we will get wounded again.'

My heart is that together we would help one another to open
up to God and allow Him to heal and restore us – bring us

back to His original intentions for us. God must first heal the broken people before He can restore the broken relationships between the artist and the Church.

From time to time I have had conversations with well known Christian musicians as they travel around. Almost without exception they have tales to tell of other musicians and artists who are hurting. Someone once said to me that the question they were most often asked by musicians was, 'Where can I go for help?'

In these days, God is giving us the knowledge and understanding so that we really **can** help. God is a very giving God – He wants to bless His children. God showed His love by giving and you can never out-give Him. God has a great lake of blessing flowing out freely from His throne and it is meant to find a reception in us. The problem is that although this lake of blessing is intended to flow upon God's children there are certain things that get in the way, such as jealousy, anger, bitterness, or unforgiveness. When we refuse to allow God to work on these areas of our life it is as if we are piling up logs that block off the flow, creating a log jam. They get in the way to the extent that instead of receiving a wonderful torrent of blessing, we only get a trickle.

One of the most difficult aspects of overcoming this 'instinct' to internalize our pain is that it is something we learn from the earliest age, and deep-seated habits are difficult to break. The more dysfunctional the family situation a person comes from, the more difficulties are wrapped up in that person. Jesuit priests say that if you give them a child before the age of seven they will give you the man. In other words a child learns by various stimuli and dynamics how to behave by the time they are seven – most of the fundamental personality traits are firmly in place.

God's desire is that everyone should be saved and come to a knowledge of the truth. The enemy however, takes great pains to build a strategy against the family, against children and many of us grow up with a distorted idea of father or mother. God intended earthly parents to be a reflection of Himself. Unfortunately, because of terrible things that happened in relation to their parents, they have not been able to parent correctly themselves, affecting their children in their most formative years. When the child grows up they carry with them the marks of their childhood.

Because of my own family background, I grew up with a pair of glasses with the word 'betrayal' written on the lenses. Everything I observed I saw through these lenses. If I couldn't trust my own father then it was easy for me to believe that other men were untrustworthy. Somehow, these kind of belief systems emanate out of a person like radio waves to others, and guess what happens? They end up being betrayed by them. It becomes a self-fulfilling prophecy – just as when Job said, *'My worst fear has come upon me.'*

The only solution to this kind of problem is to allow God to change the way we see things. I have to ask the Holy Spirit to take these glasses called **betrayal** off and put His glasses on which say **trust** so I can see correctly.

Removing the log jam

We have to find ways of removing the log jam so that the lake of blessing can flow freely. It highlights the great need that there is for inner healing and transformation. I highly recommend John and Paula Sandford's book *The Transformation of the Inner Man* [1] as the textbook on inner healing. It is a fantastic book. When you get counselors trained to counsel in this way miracles happen in people's lives. I believe inner healing is one of the keys God has given us to fulfilling His purposes. The whole subject of how our past experiences have damaged and hurt us is too vast an area for us to tackle in detail within the context of this book, but there are many helpful resources to be found. In addition to the Sandford's book, I would also recommend Dr Grant Mullen's book *Why Do I Feel So Down, When My Faith Should Lift Me Up?* [2]

A powerful evangelist had a tremendous anointing on his life. He had the sort of ministry where he could pray for people and see them healed, in fact there is documented evidence of people getting out of wheelchairs in the street. His ministry became very popular. The trouble was he was carrying with him an unresolved issue in his life that he had been repeatedly warned about. He refused to get it sorted out. Eventually, there came a time when he had built a ministry team around him and hundreds of people were following his ministry. The enemy used that unhealed area in his life – his point of weakness – to attack him. Within a three-month period he lost his ministry, his church, his wife and his children. What a tragedy! The point is that the battle is hot and the territory we are trying to reclaim is fiercely contended. The enemy will sometimes wait for years if necessary to land his planes on your landing strip and take you out. Jesus referred to this strategy of the enemy when He said, *'he* [meaning satan] *has nothing in me...'* (John 14:30).

Opening up to God

In our church we talk a lot about inner healing in the context of today's renewal and outpouring. We put a high value on lying on the floor – when God puts us there – and we like to lie there as long as we can. We put a high value on soaking in prayer and the presence of God, because the more love we experience from the Father the more capable we are of dealing with the things in our hearts. The more that we allow the things that are lodged in our hearts to be taken to the cross through repentance and forgiveness, the more we are able to experience God's love. The more we experience God's love and receive it, the more we are able to deal with the negative things – it is a virtuous circle. It is just like having a well-soaked garden where the weeds can be easily uprooted, compared to the resistance of dusty, parched, hard earth. It also makes leaders easier to follow! I believe the renewal will either grow or dwindle according to the willingness of people to be healed.

People in the past have gone so far with God and then they will go no further. If things have become uncomfortable, then maybe we have decided we are not willing to pay the price for more anointing. But without inner healing and transformation we may be running out on to the battlefield carrying a lot of baggage from our childhood. This leaves great weaknesses in our armor. Make a decision to abandon pride and allow God to do all that He wants to do in you.

A holy temple

I believe that God is calling creative people to be involved in the vanguard of prophetic intercession. Intercession begins in the heart of God. We respond to His call and invite Him to do what He has already decided to do. We have to hear His voice in order to pray what He has asked us to. David Ruis says,

> 'The intercessory cry inherent in worship must be allowed to flow. The elders are pictured falling before the throne in Revelation 5:8 with a harp (worship) in one hand and a bowl of incense (intercession) in the other. The two are inseparable, and powerful.' [3]

However, without sufficient cleansing of our hearts we may see and hear inaccurately with unhealed eyes and ears. We need to experience inner healing so that flawed character structures within us might be put to death. What I believe this means is that there is a deep wound in the hearts of mankind. This comes from the separation of Man and God at the Fall, and we are still suffering the consequences of the resulting isolation and fear (the first emotion ever mentioned in the Bible). For instance, I physically resemble my father, we all do. In the same way, all humanity resembles our spiritual ancestor, Adam. We carry the dreadful marks of inherited isolation and rejection in us, even in the womb. We don't have to learn how to feel rejected, we know already! In answer to God's question in Genesis chapter 3, *'Adam, where are you?'* Adam replied, *'I was afraid because I was naked* [without covering] *so I hid'* (Genesis 3:10). Adam made his own covering and mankind is still trying to do the same. After birth, our experiences in life all contribute, negatively or positively, to the foundation of our life. That is why all humanity desperately needs a Saviour!

A popular secular book on psychology was entitled *I'm OK, You're OK*. What it should have been called is 'I'm not OK, You're not OK, but it's OK!' J.I. Packer put it this way,

> 'The first truth is that we are all invalids in God's hospital. In moral and spiritual terms, we are all sick

and damaged, diseased and deformed, scarred and sore, lame and lopsided, to a far, far, greater extent than we realize.'[4]

If we can accept this, perhaps we can come out of hiding, trusting God to help us in our brokenness. God did not need to ask Adam where he was – He simply wanted Adam to realize where he was. Do you know where you are? God wants us to come out of hiding and be real with Him. We need to ask God into our secret hiding places and allow Him to love us back to life. In addition, anything in us which might serve as a house for the demonic has to be dealt with ruthlessly. Inner healing lays an axe to the root of the tree and once removed the enemy has no unhealed character structure in which to dwell. As we then engage in spiritual warfare, we will have no chinks in our armor that the enemy can penetrate.

Someone we love has just been taken out of ministry by the Lord because there were deep areas of wounding in him and he would not give himself to sanctification, but continued his itinerant ministry all over the world. The enemy had waited for years before blowing him up so that he could do the most damage to this man's ministry. It is an all too familiar story. You may well ask, 'How can someone minister when there is sin in their lives?' Because the gifts and the call of God are *'irrevocable and without repentance'* (Romans 11:29). We see ministers of the gospel with great anointing, still able to minister in the power of the Spirit, while bearing great character flaws. In this season God is looking for a mature army and whilst these 'unholy' areas of our lives are not dealt with, God cannot fully utilize us, and may even have to remove us from ministry for a time, if we refuse to allow God to deal with us.

Unity in the Body

Ephesians 2:20 speaks of unity in the Body of Christ and the whole Church being fitted together, growing into a holy temple in the Lord – becoming a dwelling place of God in the Spirit. Ephesians 4:3 calls us to be diligent to preserve the unity of the Spirit and calls us to be careful for the unity of the Spirit in the bond of peace. We are instructed to speak the truth in love and to grow up into Christ with each individual part working properly. This causes the Body of Christ to be built up and grow together in love. This is the vision God has for us all. What we do, the way we act and conduct ourselves affects **all of us** – the whole Body of Christ. The battle is hotting up and God is calling His army to get **cleaned up**.

Ephesians 4:22–24 goes on to say that we are to lay aside the old nature, put on the new self in God's likeness, and be renewed in our minds. This is what the ministry of inner healing is all about. Reconciliation in the body and among people, in families and among friends and between tribes and nations. It is impossible to bring about such reconciliation without repentance and forgiveness. It is the very essence of inner healing and transformation.

In John 17 Jesus prayed we would be perfected in unity so that the world would know God had sent Him. We **are** the message, and in order to represent God well we must be as like Him as possible. Can you see the direction we need to go in? We must be about the business of discipling people to bring all their hurts and problems to the cross, to help bring healing and transformation to them so they can grow up in their salvation. Jesus is coming back for a bride – one bride. His bride must be a resting place for a husband and God wants to give His son a beautiful bride. He wants her to be prepared. God's intention has always been to build 'family', and He wants to give that family the ability to rise above wounds and hurts so we are truly being 'good news' to each other and a hurting world. He doesn't want us to be broken, bruised and wounded people doing the same to our brothers and sisters as we were done to ourselves.

Amos 9:11 says that in the last days the Lord will raise up the fallen tabernacle of David. I believe that this is the restored, revived Church. A tabernacle is a dwelling place, a house for God. If you really think about it, the ultimate tabernacle is the Lord Jesus Christ Himself. God wants you and me to raise up the name of Jesus with our lives, our warfare, our intercession, our music, our genuineness and our love for Him. He wants the end-time Body of Christ – the

Church – to be such good news that the glory of God, His love and power are seen by a dying and desperate world.

Selah...

'The purpose of Christ's redeeming work was to make it possible for bad men to become good – deeply, radically, finally.'
(A.W. Tozer; 1897–1963)

'Praise the Lord, O my soul; all my inmost being, praise his holy name. Praise the Lord, O my soul, and forget not all his benefits – who forgives all your sins and heals all your diseases, who redeems your life from the pit and crowns you with love and compassion, who satisfies your desires with good things so that your youth is renewed like the eagle's.' (Psalm 103:1–5)

Notes

1. Sandford, John L. and Paula, *The Transformation of the Inner Man*, Victory House, 1982.

2. Mullen, Dr Grant, *Why Do I Feel So Down When My Faith Should Lift Me Up?*, Sovereign World, 1999.

3. From an article in *Charisma* magazine, published on Strang Communications website.

4. Packer, J.I. *Knowing God*, Intervarsity Press, 1993, pp. 65–66.

Chapter 10

Come as a Child

'Unless you come as a child...'

Observing the behavior of small children can teach us much about how we should relate to our heavenly Father. Children are so transparent – they don't hold back their feelings and are sometimes painfully honest; they always come running to their parents when they need them. Most of all they have an unfailing trust in their parents to care for them and provide for their needs. We need to learn to trust God in a childlike way too. When God had created Adam, they enjoyed fellowship together by taking a walk in the garden. Their relationship must have been relaxed and uncomplicated – a Father and His child, simply spending time together. Worship for Adam must have been a very natural and normal part of his daily life. It was as natural as breathing. The Fall robbed the generations that followed of such simplicity in worship by the introduction of sin and therefore separation. It was no longer such a straightforward exercise to enter God's presence. Thank God that through His Son, Jesus Christ, a way back has been made, and that God desires to restore simple, natural worship to our daily lives.

A.W. Tozer expressed this thought in his book *Worship, The Missing Jewel of the Evangelical Churches*. Some of the things he had to say about worship were very profound:

'Now we were made to worship, but the scriptures tell us something else again. They tell us that man fell and kept not his first estate; that he forfeited the original glory of God and failed to fulfil the creative purpose, so that he is not worshipping now in the way God meant him to worship. All else fulfils its design; flowers are still fragrant and lilies are still beautiful and the bees still search for nectar amongst the flowers; the birds still sing with their thousand voice choir on a summer's day, and the sun and the moon and the stars all move on their rounds doing the will of God.

And from what we can learn from the scriptures, we believe that the seraphim and cherubim and powers and dominions are still fulfilling their original design – worshipping God who created them and breathed into them the breath of life.

Man alone sulks in his cave. Man alone, with all of his brilliant intelligence, with all of his amazing, indescribable and wonderful equipment, still sulks in his cave.'[1]

Or as C.S. Lewis put it, man is,

'...like an ignorant child who wants to go on making mud pies in a slum because he cannot imagine what is meant by the offer of a holiday at the sea.'[2]

He is either silent, or, if he opens his mouth at all, boasts, threatens or curses. If not that, then it is nervous, ill-considered laughter; or it is humor turned into big business, or singing songs without joy. Do you feel like coming out of hiding yet?

Tozer continues,

'Man was made to worship God. God gave to man a harp and said, "Here above all the creatures I have made and created, I have given you the largest harp. I put more strings on your instrument and I have given you a wider range than I have given to any other creature. You can worship me in a manner that no other creature can." And when he sinned, man took that instrument and threw it down in the mud and there it has lain for centuries, rusted, broken, unstrung; and man, instead of playing a harp like the angels and seeking to worship

God in all his activities, is ego-centered and turns in on himself and sulks and swears and laughs and sings, but it's all without joy and without worship.'[3]

God sent His Son, Jesus, into the world for a purpose. To be a redeemer, a restorer. Part of His purpose was so that God might restore to us the missing jewel that Tozer refers to – the jewel of worship, that we might come back and learn again that which we were created to do in the first place – to worship Him in the beauty of holiness, to spend our time in awesome wonder and adoration of God; feeling and expressing it, letting it get into our work, our rest, our leisure, and doing nothing except as an act of worship to God.

Come as a child

God has decided that He is going to turn around the terrible captivity of man and even now in the nations He is building an army. This army that will be marked by worship will claim back everything that has been lost. God will restore again the tabernacle of David – the dwelling place of God. And God is working to bring us, once again, to the place where, like little children, we will trust Him, follow and obey Him, and so see His awesome power at work.

God has spoken to me a number of times about becoming more childlike, and more open to Him, but none were so poignant as three years ago when I was in the church in Toronto, and the Holy Spirit spoke to me in a most remarkable way. As a result I believe that becoming childlike before the Father is a vital key to releasing all that God intends to do in the Church through prophetic worship and intercession.

Also attending the conference in Toronto was a team of about 20 Koreans. They were all living in Los Angeles and had come over specially for the conference. They were absolutely determined to meet with God there. Korean people are very single minded. They were all very small, slim people, and even though I am sure some of them were over 30 they all looked very youthful. It is a particular blessing of the Lord on their nation that even when they are getting on in years they still look young!

During the morning meeting I found myself sitting right in the middle of them and they were doing the strangest things I have ever seen. Although they were sitting very neatly in rows, they were doing things with their hands and making signs in the air and it looked very strange. I said 'Lord, what is going on, it looks so crazy.' Suddenly one of them would get up and run around the chairs clapping her hands and acting like a small child. Another was kissing the air. I'm afraid I got offended. I said to the Lord, 'This is too much. These people have gone over the top!' So I got my coat and moved because I felt uncomfortable.

The Lord was obviously trying to show me something though, because that evening, even though we were in a church of around 5000 people, I found myself sitting in the middle of them again! I had moved, but so had they! When it came to the prayer time they all got out of their seats and ran down to the front and the Holy Spirit hit them. They all went down like ninepins in a big pile and continued to play like children, waving their arms about and laughing.

At about 11.30 pm I went up to the front of the stage and by this time there were about 20 of them lying on the floor in a heap. I noticed the lady I had seen kissing the air and I looked at her on the floor. 'Lord, this is too much,' I thought. One of the girls was saying 'Come to Jesus, come to Jesus, plenty of room, big house, big house, plenty of room for everybody, come in, come and play!' and was kissing the air again and again. I felt offended in my heart, but just then the Holy Spirit spoke to me, asking the question 'What's the matter?' 'Lord,' I said, 'Can't you see what they are doing? It's just childish!' He replied immediately, 'Yes, it is childish and I love it.' I felt my heart break at that moment because I knew how far away I was from being childlike in God's presence. All my training and experience had led me to the point where I thought I had to be a grown-up to serve God.

The Lord asked me whether I was prepared to be a child in His presence. I found it so difficult that I had a tremendous battle in my heart, because there were people from my church attending the conference with me and watching me as their pastor. I eventually said, 'Yes Lord,' took my jacket off and lay down in the middle of them, asking them to pray for me. It was the most fantastic thing I have ever done in my life. They prayed for me for $1\frac{1}{2}$ hours, about 20 of them, and I think they birthed something in my heart. They prayed for everything they could think of and there was all this signing going on. They were tapping me, touching me and absolutely assaulting me with prayer. They were praying with their bodies and their minds, throwing everything into this intercession. It wasn't dancing, singing or preaching, it was just physically interceding with everything they had. I had glimpsed intercession like I had never seen it before!

Psalm 144 says,

> *'Blessed be the Lord my rock, who trains my hand for war, and my fingers for battle.'*

God had spoken to me through that verse and I believed He was going to do it. As these Koreans were praying for me, I had the sense that God was fulfilling His word to me. I hadn't banked on the method He would use, but who am I to question Him? The thing I found my heart raging against was the fact that these people **looked** strange. It looked like they were showing off. I believe now that they were showing **forth** His glory, not showing off!

Prophetic worship

In the last 18 months or so God has started to release this same kind of prophetic intercession into some churches. I believe it is a direct result of childlike obedience. My wife Ze, who is not a musician, has lately started to come on stage with me, and as I am leading worship she is standing behind me. She said to me after one Sunday morning meeting that she wanted to intercede for me while I was leading worship. She felt we were going to experience particularly intense spiritual warfare and she wanted to do battle on my behalf. Encouraged by our friends, Lawrence and Sarah Bernstein, I asked her to come on the stage with me and do what God had told her to do. I had borrowed a guitar which had no strap button, so I was sitting on a high stool to lead the worship. Ze came up behind me and as soon as she touched me and started to intercede for me my mind cleared, the level of anointing in the room went up at least 60% and the Holy Spirit came in great power. I felt that my spirit and my wife's spirit had been welded together.

That afternoon Ze and I had lunch with my keyboard player and we sat together for three hours like teenage sweethearts. It was one of the most liberating experiences we have ever had. I had invited my wife into that private place where she could not come before because she was not a musician. She told me later that God had given her specific instructions during the hour of worship. She knew she had to build a 'booth' of prayer. As she was praying she saw in the spirit part of the roof cave in and she had to build it again. She stood for the whole hour behind me using her hands to intercede for me. It released me to fight with music and with song. I won't lead worship now without her being there.

God has put us together strongly in a new way. I don't know how it works for those who are not married, but I know God is calling the intercessors and worship leaders to be one in the spirit. Take your intercessors into your worship meetings and your worship musicians into your intercessory prayer meetings and release the prophetic. Don't have any barriers in your mind about what is acceptable and right and proper, but allow the Lord to do it. This is something new in the earth. At Rick Joyner's church in Charlotte, USA called Morningstar, the worship leader's wife is doing the same thing.

David Ruis said in a *Charisma* magazine article,

'One cannot address the issue of the arts and worship without acknowledging its connection in the Scriptures to the prophetic. As David released musicians in the tabernacle, they were encouraged to prophesy in voice as well as on instruments (1 Chronicles 15:22; 25:1). When Elisha was cornered into prophesying for Jehoshaphat, he couldn't even begin without a musician present (2 Kings 3:15). In the New Testament, it was as prophets were gathered in Antioch that we find them worshipping the Lord and fasting (Acts 13:1–2).'

Healing worship

Childlike, open, transparent worshippers of the Father will also move in 'healing worship' as God moves through them by His Spirit. David Ruis, commenting on our corporate worship, says:

> 'Whatever our liturgy, whether our "presentation" has been crafted or is spontaneous, we must ask the Holy Spirit to release His prophetic oil on our creativity. Then we will see freedom and healing in our worship.'

1 Samuel 16:14–23 tells the story of Saul, tormented by an evil spirit, calling for an anointed musician to come and do warfare on his behalf. This is another example of the Psalm 144 principle that David wrote about – the Lord training hands for war, fingers for battle. I am making a distinction between hands used in intercession and fingers playing an instrument. There was tremendous deliverance when David started to praise God in this instrumental way. It is an example of a particular type of warfare. When we play our instruments, God breathes through them and sings through them. When demons hear it they are driven out. This is what the agents of Lucifer were particularly concerned about closing down during the Dark Ages of the Church's history. During that period there was so much bloodshed and cruelty on the earth it was almost as if the demons were in charge.

David drove away the demons in Saul with anointed and skilful playing. When you play your instrument, know that the enemy is fleeing seven ways from you (Deuteronomy 28:7). If you have musicians in your church, anoint them and their instruments, lay your hands on the instruments and dedicate them as holy things to the Lord for Him to sing through, to invade the spirit of the musician and breathe out deliverance. It is an incredibly powerful thing – please don't allow it to be shut down. You need to pray for your musicians, to encourage them to get better at what they do. We are discovering there are different sounds that God likes, not just stringed instruments, but also percussive instruments – sounds to fill the air with praise and worship.

I have in my possession a new electric double-bass, which not only makes a great sound, but is also a great work of art. It was invented by Mike Anderson,[4] a Christian living in Scotland! I believe there are other instruments still to come, things that we have never seen, yet to be invented. Maybe such instruments will cover more of the electro-magnetic spectrum and will use light as well as sound! Who can put boundaries on the creativity of God, breathed into a man? Who can put boundaries on the possibilities of healing power, released through creative, prophetic and intercessory worship?

Selah...

'Children possess an uncanny ability to cut to the core of an issue, to expose life to the bone, and strip away the barnacles that cling to the hull of our too sophisticated pseudo-civilization. One reason for this, I believe, is that children have not mastered our fine art of deception that we call "finesse". Another is that they are so "lately come from God" that faith and trust are second nature to them. They have not acquired the obstructions to faith that come with education; they possess instead unrefined wisdom, a gift from God.' (Gloria Gaither)

Father I pray that you would help us to become more childlike in our walk before you, so that you will be able to release true prophetic and healing worship among us – we hunger and thirst for this to happen. Let it come in our churches, raise up intercession and let it mingle with the prophetic. Remove our own puny ideas of what is acceptable to You God and help us to be humble enough to see new things.

Notes

1. Tozer, A.W., *Worship, The Missing Jewel of the Evangelical Church*, Pennsylvania, Christian Publications Inc., 1961, p. 11.

2. Lewis, C.S. *The Weight of Glory and Other Addresses*, edited by Walter Hooper, Touchstone Books, 1996.

3. Ibid., p. 12.

4. Mike Anderson can be contacted by email at:
   mike@starfishdesign.co.uk

*'Come from the four winds, O breath,
and breathe into these slain,
that they may live.'*

(Ezekiel 37:9)

SECTION 2

Glory Recaptured

If we allow God to shape our
character, our gifts will flourish.
Worshippers have always been warriors,
and warriors have always been worshippers.
The result of our co-operation with God will be:
Prophetic worship;
Healing worship;
Worship warfare;
An increasing anointing.
The more whole we become in Christ,
the more God will be able to release
His blessing through us to
following generations.

Chapter 11

The Artist's Spiritual Ancestry

The curse of the Fall

Throughout the first section of this book we have discussed the fact that the Church has been robbed of the richness of variety and creativity that it should be enjoying through the ministry of creative artists. We have also established that God is determined to restore and heal the broken relationships that have occurred between the Church and the artistic fraternity, and that in order to do this He must first heal broken individuals. In this next section we will examine some of the manifestations that will increasingly result from this process – prophetic worship, healing worship, increasingly effective intercession and a greater anointing in worship. But before we look forward, allow me to take one last look back.

I believe that an essential part of understanding who we are is to examine our past. Looking back to what our ancestors did and what they were like will provide vital clues to our own behavior. This has certainly proved invaluable for those involved in counseling others in practical matters of repeated, generational sin, but will also help us to understand our spiritual heritage as creative artists.

Genesis chapter 4 tells us the very poignant story of Cain, son of Adam and Eve. It illustrates very well how a person can be affected by their parents' actions and be diverted from their true purpose. Adam and Eve were responsible for populating the earth and subduing it. They were meant to have complete dominion over the earth. Eve, however, believed the lie of satan and questioned God's advice. She wanted to get good things off the 'forbidden' tree but did not ask her husband's advice first. He too went against God's advice and listened to his wife instead. He then made it worse by blaming his wife. In order to protect them, God had to send them away from the garden, away from the tree of life.

As they left the garden however, the seeds of rejection were already sown. The glory had departed from them. They no longer had any defense and they saw they were naked. They both sewed fig leaves to cover themselves up, but even though He had to send them away from the garden, God still had compassion on them and made them leather coats from animal skins to wear instead. The killing of these animals to provide a covering foreshadowed the blood sacrifice that we now see in the atonement of Jesus that covers our sin. God was showing Adam and Eve that in spite of their rejection of His laws and their rebellion and sin, He still cared for them.

The seeds of rejection were now sown. Rejection means to discard something as not wanted. It is a refusal of love. Even though they had left the garden God still loved them but they refused to accept His love. The Bible does not tell us that they went back to God and asked Him what could be done to restore things. We don't know what would have happened if either of them had been able to ask for forgiveness.

Cain – born under the curse

Now living outside the glory and presence of God, Adam and Eve have children. The principles of God come into play and the children are born in their father's and mother's likeness – just as they were created in His. Generationally they are born into a situation where they are under a curse. They are not born in the likeness of God but the likeness of Adam and Eve.

Their first-born son was called Cain and the second was called Abel. Cain became a gardener like Adam and Abel became a shepherd. When they were both quite young Cain brought God an offering and it was a product of Cain's own hard work. Cain had followed in Adam's footsteps and worked hard at growing things. God rejected his offering because it was based on works, but Abel brought a first-born lamb, a blood sacrifice, with which God was pleased. Cain was angry, indignant, sad and depressed. In Genesis 4:6–7 the Lord asked him why he was angry and told him that sin was crouching at his door but he should master it. In other words, God said to Cain if he carried on like this he would become consumed with sin and be co-operating with the devil. Cain became very jealous of his brother and murdered him. God explained to Cain that he was now cursed himself because he had spilled innocent blood. Cain was exiled and made his lot worse by complaining and rebelling against God. The seeds of rejection inherited from his parents were now fully grown in Cain and giving forth their harvest.

Cain's destiny

As we have previously discussed, a person's name usually carries the sense of 'who they are' and is often more than just an arbitrary title. A study of the names of the generations coming down from Adam and Eve is very interesting for this reason. What was Cain's destiny in God according to his name? It meant variously 'first-born', 'a lance or spear', 'a teacher of how to raise cattle', 'to provoke to jealousy' and 'to redeem or recover'. I would interpret that to mean that Cain's true, God-given purpose as the first-born, was to be the redeemer of the situation that his mother and father created. That is what God had called him. He was to teach men how to raise cattle and to recover what had been lost as a successful man. His destiny was to be sent forth as a spear to provoke jealousy unto God.

What Cain actually became he inherited spiritually from his parents. He was implanted with the seed of rejection and by his choices it produced its fruit in his life. Cain is sad, angry, depressed and rebellious, indignant and jealous. He did not even start to fulfill his destiny. He should have been a teacher of how to keep cattle, yet he became a grower of crops and eventually a murderer. He destroyed his destiny by his choices. It is possible for you to do that too.

Cain then carries on his own family line and has several sons. He has a son called Enoch, whose name means 'a patriarch', 'to dedicate', and 'to train up', but also means 'to strangle yourself'. He had a son called Irad, meaning 'a fugitive', and 'somebody who is isolated'. He also had a son called Mehujael – a very interesting name because it means 'Who is God?' and this was only four generations away from Adam and Eve, his great grandparents who had actually walked with God in the Garden!

Jubal – father of musicians

Mehujael himself had two sons. One named Methushael and Lamech. Having sown the seeds himself earlier, murder repeats itself in Cain's family line. Genesis 4:23 reveals that Lamech killed a man for wounding him. Lamech married two women. His first wife was called Adah and her name means 'an ornament', or 'to adorn oneself', and she was probably very pretty. Lamech and Adah had two sons, the first was called Jabal, who is said to be the father of tent dwellers and merchants.

Their second son was called Jubal. He was the father of everybody who plays the harp and lyre (Genesis 4:21) – in other words the father of musicians. Here you have two brothers, Jabal who dwelled in isolation and was always on the move, never settling in one place, and Jubal who was the father of musicians. If you are a musician then Jubal is your ancestral father. He is linked with his brother who has wanderlust in his heart, never wanting to stay in one place, and this is the spiritual ancestry of anyone who plays an instrument in your church. Whether these people want it or not, they are cursed with anger and jealousy. That may shock some, and yet if the truth is told, every one of us has listened to a really talented person playing the same instrument as we do at one time or another, and found it difficult not to hate them.

We have anger and jealousy in our hearts and are under a curse until we allow the Lord to deal with us. We have to recognize our weaknesses before the Lord and cry out to the Holy Spirit to help us. Whether you want this curse or not it is in your heart. We try to deal with this situation in our own strength by getting better at what we do and performing. In the days when early jazz trumpet players used to have a 'battle' to see who was the best, some of them used to put a handkerchief over their hands so nobody could see the fingering they were using. They would not help each other, but would compete fiercely, and were often jealous of others' talents. This attitude is coming directly down your spiritual ancestral line and needs dealing with!

Although we put so much emphasis on trying to improve our performance, the time is coming when Jesus is not going to tolerate mere performance in His house any more. Historically, for Jewish people, the word 'theater' had serious connotations. For them it meant a place of judgement. The Greek influence changed that. They made 'theater' into a light-hearted, satirical and comical thing. They turned a place of judgement into a place of entertainment. Along with many other aspects of Greek thought and influence, we too seem to have inherited this same spirit. We have a desire to be entertained and have decided that the anointing that God desires is just too uncomfortable – too costly. We want to entertain people to make them feel better so they will praise us. We are receiving our praise from man. There are people in our churches who would rather be entertained by us than pay the price of the glory of God. All the time we are standing on the stage and enjoying the applause of people we have jealousy and murder in our hearts for our brothers who play better than we do – whose offering is better than ours.

Make a decision today, that you will deal ruthlessly with any unresolved issues concerning both your natural and spiritual ancestry. There is no jealousy in your veins that the blood of Jesus is not able to cleanse. There is no curse He is unable to break, because He became a curse for us. All He needs is a response from you and then He can set you free.

Our Levitical heritage

Although, as creative artists we were born into this world in sin, and so were aligned with the spiritual heritage of those who sinned in the Garden, when we are born again in Christ, we become identified with a new and more powerful spiritual heritage – one which God intended for us all along. Instead of being the jealous, hostile, introverted, wandering children of Jubal and Jabal, we can function as the sanctified, anointed, worshipping Levitical priests that minister before God's throne. In order to do this, we need to allow God to purify and refine us. Malachi 3:2–5 says this:

> *'For he is like a refiner's fire and a fullers' soap; He will sit as a refiner and a purifier of silver, he will purify the sons of Levi and refine them like gold and silver, till they present right offerings to the Lord. Then the offering of Judah and Jerusalem will be pleasing to the Lord as in the days of old and as in former years. "Then I will draw near to you for judgement; I will be a swift witness against the sorcerers, the adulterers, against those who swear falsely, against those who oppress the hireling in his wages, the widow and orphan, against those who thrust aside the sojourners, and do not fear me," says the Lord.'*

When there are Levites who are committed to being absolutely pure and are bringing pure offerings to God, then God says, *'I will draw near to you for judgement.'* The Lord will judge the sin of your city and allow you to use the sword of the Lord against demonic powers that are holding people in bondage all around you. As the Levitical warriors offer pure worship to the Lord, He will dwell amongst them and His presence will be powerfully manifest. As Tommy Tenney says in his book *The God Chasers*, 'We have seen what happens when God visits a church, but not when He visits a city.' I believe that as more and more creative artists realize the call to their Levitical heritage, whole cities and regions **will** be impacted by the manifest presence of God, drawing people to repentance. John and Paula Sandford have this to add,

> 'Those who are at rest in the Father's love can be used by Him to work untold wonders of healing throughout the nations ... by burden bearing intercession. Imagine what could happen in every region and country if the Lord were to raise up an elite corps of adept burden

bearers – intercessory prayer warriors. How much misery could be eased, what changes would take place among religious, political and ethnic groups. How much healing of the nations might result?'[1]

The central function of the Levitical worshipper is to cover the throne of God with praise, and make himself available for 'burden bearing' intercession (the concept of burden bearing is explained more fully in Chapter 13). When this happens we share the Lord's pain for the city and literally **feel** the pain of the lost people who occupy it. Sensing the sin in their lives, we actually **become** intercession for them.

God is listening and waiting for the lost music and the lost musicians who will separate themselves from everything that defiles them, and offer pure offerings of worship to Him. When He hears the beautiful sounds and recognizes the purified hearts and commitment to wholeness in the players and singers, and when He sees the clouds of fragrant intercession rising before Him like incense, He will not be able to resist joining in, much like the picture Jesus presented to us of a father rushing to greet his wayward son.

Selah...

'Let all bitterness and indignation and wrath (passion, rage, bad temper) and resentment (anger, animosity) and quarrelling (brawling, clamor, contention) and slander (evil-speaking, abusive or blasphemous language) be banished from you, with all malice (spite, ill will, or baseness of any kind). And become useful and helpful and kind to one another, tenderhearted (compassionate, understanding, loving-hearted), forgiving one another (readily and freely), as God in Christ forgave you.'

(Ephesians 4:31–32 Amplified Bible)

Note

1. Sandford, John L. and Paula, *The Healing of the Nations*, Victory House, 1999.

Chapter 12

Worship as Warfare

The spirit of Jehoshaphat

2 Chronicles 20 tells us a wonderful story about King Jehoshaphat, who was been pretty smart because he was always asking for musicians! Maybe he was one himself. He had a problem with the Ammonites and somebody had come to tell him that *'...a great multitude,'* – the Ammonites and several other allies – were coming against him to take him out. Jehoshaphat was afraid and told his people to fast and seek the Lord together.

The whole of Judah sought the Lord and Jehoshaphat prayed fervently because he had no strategy and did not know what to do. The Spirit of the Lord came on a musician, a Levite called Jahaziel, and gave him a word for Jehoshaphat. He told him that the battle was not his, it belonged to the Lord. He would not need to fight in the battle, but just to position himself, stand still, and observe the salvation of the Lord who was with him. Jehoshaphat appointed those who should sing to the Lord and praise the beauty of His Holiness and they went out ahead of the army. When they began to sing and praise, the Lord made toast of the enemy! The victory was won by using worship and praise to God as warfare.

Worship and spiritual warfare

This principle was painfully illustrated to me several years ago, but the result was that I learned an important lesson in using worship in warfare just as Jehoshaphat did. I also learnt the importance of having proper spiritual authority in place as a church leader. Allow me to explain:

In 1991 I was leading worship at a weekend youth camp when I felt the Spirit of the Lord encouraging me to become more militant in my worship. I was very excited by this and went home determined to get more aggressive in our praise because we wanted to see the church move on in the power of the Spirit and needed all hindrances to God's blessing removed. I was leading worship the following Sunday evening and as I was worshipping the Lord I declared to the people that we were going into battle – that there were things that God wanted to do with the church.

At this time we did not have our own building; we were renting a school and there were only about 150 of us. We had not really established ourselves in the city. I felt that God wanted to establish His presence in the community and do all sorts of new things with us. I knew that we would stay where we were for years unless something happened. I stood up that Sunday night and said 'All those who are with me stand and let's declare before the Lord that we are going into battle. I will lead you.' We had an exciting meeting and everyone was very enthusiastic about what God was going to do.

Crisis point

I went to bed that night and rose at around 5.30 am in the morning to go to the bathroom. I discovered I had a tingling sensation of 'pins and needles' in my arm and leg. I thought perhaps I had lain in an awkward way in the night, so I went back to bed and fell asleep again. I woke up again at about 8.30 am and my wife said to me, 'Are you OK?' I said that I thought I was, but she insisted that I should go and see a doctor. I went to dial his number and as I spoke to him, realized that I was slurring my words and still had pins and needles in my arm. He came round at once and diagnosed that I had suffered a stroke during the night. The feeling in my arm, side, face and leg didn't come back.

I went to see a specialist that day and he confirmed that I had suffered a stroke. When we saw the X-ray we were amazed. A tiny blood clot had occurred in a very small area, and yet with almost pinpoint accuracy it had completely taken away the ability to play my instrument. When the specialist told me I wept and was very distressed. I told him I was a musician and he told me I would just have to live without playing and that I would never be the same again.

When I prayed with Ze about it I felt such anger rising up inside me. The very thing that God had encouraged me to do – engage in militant worship warfare – the enemy was attacking strongly. The next Sunday I stood before the church with my hand in my pocket so people could not see how bad it was, even though I was dragging my leg on he floor. I was so angry with the enemy, but at the same time realized that I absolutely believed the Lord was willing to heal me. We prayed about it constantly for a month, but nothing happened. All I could do was ask the Lord, 'Why?'

We then discovered that there was a deep division in the church leadership of that time. For some time a senior leader had been speaking against me in private and the church had started to be divided over my leadership. It was very subtle, and on the surface appeared to be reasonable, but was division nonetheless. This was a painful discovery, but for the time being my main concern was to get my own body back into shape. I realized that my spirit was not able to receive the healing God wanted to give me at that time. Ze and I set out on a strict time of discipline to try to increase the capacity to receive healing. I asked the Lord for a strategy and we started to fast and to pray. I joined a heath club, lost weight, and changed my diet in order to improve all the purely physical aspects of the situation that I could. Then I entered into a regime of doing three or four Bible studies a day, listening to tapes and constantly feeding my spirit with the Word of God. I constantly thanked Him for my healing and spoke out the Word of God as I worshipped.

We took a rest from the church but in the April of that year I had been booked to lead worship at a large Christian festival. I was sure God was going to heal me but we were already into January and it still hadn't happened. So I had to ring John Menlove, my keyboard player, and say I couldn't do the job.

When I told him what had happened to me he was shocked. He called me back a week later and said he had booked another worship leader but he couldn't find a bass player. He asked **me** to play the bass! I said, 'I can't even hold it, let alone play it!' But he said he had been praying about it and God had told him to ask me. I said I would pray about it also and God told me to take the job! 'I don't know how I am going to do this,' I thought, but I rang him up and agreed.

When I arrived at the camp, I set up and turned on my amplifier as normal, sat in a chair and managed to play one note in every three for the first week. On the Thursday of the second week I was still thanking God for my healing when all of a sudden, with nobody near me, feeling started to come back into my shoulder. It felt like a tap of warm water being turned on! I could feel it trickling down my arm, down my left side, into my leg and foot. I thought, 'God you are healing me!' and I started to cry. 'What's happening?' the drummer asked as I started to play better. I got 70% of my feeling back that night. At last I believe my spirit was able to receive that night what God had wanted to give me all the time. After that I began to do exercises to build up my strength again. I give God the glory.

The Jezebel spirit

Why was the enemy able to attack me in such a strong way? Ze and I realized that it was because a spirit of division had entered our church. This spirit was the 'Jezebel' spirit – concerned with trying to shut down the prophetic with false authority. How had it found an entry into our church? Because the proper order of spiritual authority was not in balance. The historical Jezebel thrived because Ahab, her husband and the king – the rightful authority – was a weak man who would not bring discipline and allowed his wife to control him. A similar situation had arisen in my church too. My trusted leader had seemed a very capable person. He had done a few things that I had not really agreed with, and I wasn't 100% sure that they were the Lord's will, but because he seemed to know what he was doing I let them go without correcting him and I let this thing grow. That was my sin and when I went before the Lord, repented and asked Him what to do, I got no quick and easy answer.

I spoke to the Lord saying, 'This man says that he is the pastor, not me. Well if you want to give him this church I will bless and release him into it and I will go and do something else.' The Lord said to me 'What did I ask you to do?' and He reminded me that He had made me the pastor. At that point I realized I had to go back and take the reins – God's desired spiritual order must be restored. The problem was that this Jezebel spirit had really invaded the church, and like unseen tentacles, it had crept into almost every department. I was really frightened and thought 'How on earth am I going to turn this thing around?'

I eventually realized that because it was a spirit coming against us that the battle was to be won in the spiritual realms with spiritual weapons. The Bible describes the role of the Levite in Exodus 32:26–28, not just as someone who would to bring beauty and pleasure to the Lord, but also to bring judgement. They were warriors as well as worshippers – or Worship Warriors!

When Moses came down from the mountain and saw the people dancing before the golden calf it was the Levites he called on to draw their swords against their brothers and bring judgement in the camp. If you have been called to stand in the office of a Levite and have agreed to do it, you must know that you may be called upon to execute judgement and authority over spirits. This is what God instructed me to do.

I fasted for ten days and asked God what to do and God gave me a strategy. I knew I had to stand in my strongest anointing. I had stood before my church about three months earlier and told them I was going to take some time out to go and look for my healing, and when I had been healed and regained my strength I was going after the very thing that the enemy had sought to take away from me. It was time for me to go forward in militant worship.

Spiritual authority

I told my leaders I was going to come against the Jezebel spirit by taking certain actions. At that point the church had divided into three and there were seeds of rebellion in the camp. God had told me that I was to call back in the southern 'branch' that had gone out from the church so that we would be united again, and I told my congregation so. Some were horrified, but I knew for certain that God was with me and I had His word to do it. So, right in the middle of the worship, when everyone was singing praise to God, I said 'In the name of Jesus, the south branch is coming in next week and I come against that Jezebel spirit in the name of Jesus and command you to leave.' After that we got into some warfare praise. There were some shocked faces in the church, and I certainly don't recommend doing this unless you have had a clear word from the Lord! But since that time the church has gone from strength to strength and nobody ever questioned my leadership authority from that point on. I don't have to make a big thing of it either; there is a lot of freedom and blessing, people are getting saved and the ministry is very fruitful. Whatever situation you find yourself in, remember this: powerful spirits can be defeated through worship when you are operating under God's authority.

The importance of operating from a position of God-given authority cannot be emphasized enough. A lady asked me once – having seen that my wife was standing behind me during worship – 'Is it valid for ladies to be worship leaders?' (Following the model we have adopted, maybe their husbands would also stand behind them?) My advice to her was this: Galatians 3:26–28 says '... *there is neither male nor female; for you are all one in Christ Jesus.*' If, as a woman, God has given you a ministry of praise and worship and put the spirit of a leader on you, then you have to find yourself a situation where you can exercise that gift, and where you are given the freedom to be a leader. I do not want to upset pastors and leaders who may have a problem with this, but at the same time we do not want this gift to be shut down. The key is God's calling. If the desire to lead worship has been born out of God's call on your life, then He will make room for you to function. If God has not called you to such a position of leadership, then every attempt to make it happen on your own will be frustrated. When God gives someone the authority to function in a particular role, you obstruct them at your peril!

If you want God to minister through you, then you must work under proper authority and belong to a team that supports what you are doing and is able to release you into your gift. I personally have never had any problem with women leaders; in fact my wife is the co-pastor of our home church, but someone has to take ultimate responsibility and that falls to me. Ze and I have equal authority and responsibility in the church, but I am the one God is going to hold responsible if He is going to adjust anything. My wife receives revelation and I need to make sure that I listen to her. I would be stupid not to, I find God in her, and she has so much wisdom in the Lord. But, I believe I will be answerable for what goes on in my church as I am answerable for what goes on in my household.

If God has given you a gift and a calling and you don't move into it, God will not get what He deserves and there will be churches and ministries that will be poorer as a result.

Hearing from God

Recognizing and respecting spiritual authority in its proper place will ultimately protect you from vulnerability. I was once invited to go and minister in Holland. The gist of their invitation ran something like this:

> '40 years ago T.L. Osborne came to this country and started a revival. This month is the 40th anniversary of his visit. The Rolling Stones will be playing here the weekend before on their "Bridges to Babylon" tour, and the name of the shopping mall where we are holding our meetings is called "Babylon". Please come and minister and bring a word from the Lord.'

I didn't want to go after hearing that! But, I prayed about it and the Lord said to go. I really did not want to go as 'God's man for the hour' – I knew I could have spent hours waiting for a word and never getting one.

In prayer, the Lord reminded me of a passage in 2 Kings

chapter 3 where a group of kings were intending to go out to battle and were looking for guidance. They went to see Elisha the prophet because they realized that before they went into battle they had to have a word from the Lord. They were worried about being wiped out. When they approached the prophet Elisha he knew they were coming to him for a word. Sometimes we can get under tremendous pressure when we are asked to 'come up with something'. Elisha wisely asked for a musician. When the musician played, the hand of the Lord came upon Elisha and he was able to instruct them.

I went to minister at this church. I told them I was not going to bring a word from the Lord, but that I would come and play and that God would speak to the leadership. This took the pressure off. They were the ones with the authority and responsibility for their church. I helped them hear from the Lord so they would come up with a strategy that they could follow through and be responsible for.

Never overstep your authority and allow the enemy to draw you out. If you feel you have a word for the church you are in, pray about it and if the word persists ask your pastor if you can give him the word. If he says yes, write it down and give it to him, but once you have done this leave it there. It is his responsibility to follow up, not yours, and if he feels it is not right to bring it right away, please don't get upset – just leave it in the Lord's hands.

The issue of spiritual authority is vital for the worship leader. As far as the worship leader is concerned, whether the pastor is a musician or not (and therefore perceived in the eyes of the musicians as having a greater or lesser understanding of what they are doing), he must still be respected and recognized as the 'chief worshipper' in the church – ultimately responsible to God for what happens. The pastor is the one with the authority from God to direct what happens in the church and the worship leader has delegated authority from him – even if the pastor thinks a crotchet is something to do with knitting! The fact that the worship leader may be a highly accomplished musician and the leader is not, does not negate the pastor's position as chief worshipper. Jeremy Sinnott, in his book *An Audience of One*[1] makes this point well, commenting on 1 Chronicles

25:1–7, when King David appointed various musicians for ministry in the House of the Lord:

> 'The line of authority was clearly defined. David, the king, just happened to be a musician, but it was his kingly authority that was the important issue here. In other words, the leader of our congregation, namely the pastor, has authority over the worship ministry, regardless of whether or not he is a musician ... It is also very interesting that the commanders of the army chose musicians. Again, these officers were probably not musicians themselves, but they had a position of authority over the musicians they chose.'

Again the link is defined between worship and warfare. In short, God is restoring the musical Levite to the Church. When King David brought the Ark of the Covenant back to Jerusalem, only the Levites were anointed for that task. It had to be done properly. That's why Uzzah died, trying to steady the 'presence of God' as it was being brought into the city on a cart – he was not equipped or anointed for that job. One of King David's priorities was to sanctify the Levites – to get them 'cleaned up' so that they could offer 'clean' worship to the Lord (Malachi 3:2–5). When people offer up that kind of worship, God visits the people with His presence and a 'visitation' happens, God is enthroned on the praise of His people. Who knows what would happen if the presence of God came into our cities as it did in David's day. This is where the Church **must** go. Imagine what will happen when 'cleaned up', sanctified, anointed Levitical musicians and singers make themselves available to God to breath through them in secular music venues right in the middle of our cities and towns!

The commanders of God's army recognized the power that worship would play in any ensuing battles. The Levitical warrior-worshippers would play a central role in their military campaigns, and so shall we play our part in the advance of God's kingdom when we function in our God-given roles under the correct, God-given authority.

Selah...

'The Lord takes pleasure in his people; he honors the humble with victory. Let God's people rejoice in their triumph and sing joyfully all night long. Let them shout aloud as they praise God, with their sharp swords in their hands to defeat the nations and to punish the peoples; to bind their kings in chains of iron; to punish the nations as God has commanded. This is the victory of God's people. Praise the Lord!'   (Psalm 149:4–9 GNB)

Note

1. Sinnott, Jeremy – *An Audience of One*, Destiny Image, Shippensburg, USA, 1999, p.63.

Chapter 13

Burden Bearing

'Bear one another's burdens and so fulfil the law of Christ.'
(Galatians 6:2)

One of the things I have discovered is that my own spirit is very different to my wife's. I am not simply talking about the differences between men and women, but how our spirits accept and deal with things. My wife has a very buoyant spirit, it's always up, always very light and she is always a very happy person. She is joyful and always encouraging. While she is sensitive to other people's hurt and pain she is seldom actually depressed.

We were on holiday in America recently. I had no work to do and all we had was a beautiful beach to lie on for five days. I had no worries to take care of, no responsibilities. The sunsets were fantastic, the food was lovely and the sea was very warm, but I was very depressed and didn't know why. My wife looked at me and said, 'What's the matter with you? You have absolutely nothing to worry about, everything is going well.'

I said, 'I don't know. I don't seem able to be as buoyant as you are about things; things sit on me and it takes me a long time to recover.'

I believe that these differences in spiritual temperament result from the fact that I am a **burden bearer** and my wife is not – at least not in the sense that we will discuss here. I came to this conclusion through studying the pioneering teaching of our friends, John and Paula Sandford, and through various extremely enlightening conversations with John regarding burden bearing. Furthermore, I believe that a great many creative artists are burden bearers – so what exactly is one?

We need to come to an understanding of the fact that, as artists, we are involved in worship that is to cover the throne of God. But while we seek to worship and express what is on God's heart through prophetic intercession, we also pick up and carry the pains, hurts and needs of the people present, **back** into God's presence. As Levites – priestly worshippers – we are like connections to God's presence; a connection from God to the people, and from the people to God. The Holy Spirit of God moves through the worship music to touch the people and minister to them. Sometimes He dislodges hurt and sorrow in their lives and the Lord draws it to Himself, to the cross to be dealt with. The point is that the musician is the channel, God is drawing it through you, back to Himself. Many worship leaders will tell you that when they leave the stage, maybe having had a wonderful experience of the presence of God, they sometimes feel 'defiled' and vulnerable. The only plausible explanation is that God has allowed them to be the channel through which He draws out the peoples' sin and pain.

Paul understood this principle and spoke about it in 2 Corinthians 4:10 when he described himself as,

> '... *always carrying about in the body the dying of the Lord Jesus, that the life of Jesus also may be manifested in our body. For we who live are always delivered to death for Jesus' sake, that the life of Jesus also may be manifested in our mortal flesh. So then death is working in us, but life in you.'*

2 Corinthians 4:10 is what happens to musicians and creative people. God puts the musician, the artist, the worship leader in front to lead the people. God then pours life through the music into the people. It enters into them and draws the death – burdens, grief, pain, sorrow, even wild sexual impulses – everything – back through the musician to the Lord's cross.

If a musician does not understand what is happening, then he or she can become weighed down with the emotional baggage of others in the room, without knowing how to hand those burdens over to the Lord. They can be filled with impulses from other people and not realize that they are not coming from within. This explains why so many musicians come off the stage feeling like doing something crazy, and have so much unreleased energy inside them. I also believe that this is why so many worship leaders have become burned-out and have gone off the rails, eventually crumpling under the burden that they couldn't find any outlet for.

I believe that burden bearing has also brought about the demise of many non-Christian musicians and artists. They have no idea of where they might release all the emotional baggage that they absorb. This explains to me why so many have turned to drugs to try and dull the pain of these impulses and feelings. I believe that musicians like Hendrix who overdosed on drugs, and Kurt Cobain who committed suicide, failed to work out how to deal with the burdens of the people they sought to speak to through music. How could they possibly cope with the deadly cocktail of defilement combined with the aching frustration of the lack of God's glory in their lives?

For years the highest rate of suicide was among psychiatrists, because in an attempt to heal people they were carrying peoples' burdens – taking it upon themselves to absorb all the emotional energy, yet without knowing how to 'burden bear'. The same is true for musicians and worship leaders. God delivers us to death for Jesus' sake so that death is at work in us, but life is at work in others.

As artists and musicians I believe God designed us to be burden bearers and intercessors. He created artists, musicians, painters, actors and dancers to represent the people before God and God before the people.

My wife often used to say to me, 'What's the matter with you? You've done a great gig and earned a lot of money, you're doing everything you ever hoped and dreamed of, so why are you so depressed?' My reply to her was always, 'I don't know!' I want to tell you that I have now found what I've been looking for: it is the glory of God, the presence of Jesus! The presence of God makes all the difference.

One day while we were discussing this principle of burden

bearing, my friend John Sandford told me about one of his own experiences. A woman came in to see him for counseling. Even if he had been vulnerable, she wasn't really 'his type' and he didn't find her very attractive, but as he was counseling her, he started to have lustful thoughts about her. He said it was difficult as he had to look interested in what she was saying, but all the time he had this warning light saying 'Danger'. He asked God what was going on and the Lord told him to ask her a question. He asked the woman if she had been thinking lustful thoughts about him and she admitted it. What was happening was that he was burden bearing, receiving those messages, empathizing with her, and it became defilement when his mind translated it as his own feelings.

A group of witches were converted to Christianity. One of them was a beautiful young woman who had been delivered and cleaned up by the Lord. She went along to church and was suddenly filled with impure thoughts and lustful images again. She went for counseling thinking that she must still be demonized, but the counselor could not discern any demonic activity at all. After a few minutes the Lord revealed that the young man she had sat next to was lusting after her and she was burden bearing. His 'death' was working death in her. She had not understood this and thought it was her own feelings.

A final story to further illustrate the outworking of burden bearing is the choir director who had been directing professionally for 30 years. Every so often she would take an amateur choir and try to train them. The people she was training were not very competent musically and lacked confidence. When she was standing in front of them, the thought came into her mind that she didn't know what she was doing – how to read music, how to keep time – and she lost her own confidence. The she realized she had been burden bearing. This was how the choir felt and she was identifying with them, thinking that the feelings were her own. It had become burden bearing defilement.

When musicians are standing in front of a congregation, all the 'stuff' from fallen personalities is coming through them and they often think it is them. Think about music having the capacity to amplify the spirit of man. Now imagine being at a rock concert where the Holy Spirit is not in control. Is it possible that all the 'bad stuff' gets amplified? Think about the scenario in heaven with Lucifer. It is possible that he allowed himself to be filled up with all the amazing worship of the other angels that was actually intended for God Himself, and allowed it to become the source of his pride and arrogance.

He led the worship for all the angels to sing and worship God. All the glory was flowing through him, being amplified, until he began to think that he was something awesome. He liked it so much he wanted to keep it for himself instead of releasing it to God. He is stood in his role as an intercessor, locking into the worship of all the angelic hosts and began to imagine that it was him they were worshipping. He was deceived, and indeed is the father of deception.

Now think about your role as a worshipping artist. It is a very vulnerable position to be in. What steps can we take to protect ourselves? It is important that we take action, especially in these days when the Lord is clearly calling the Church back to real holiness, because the enemy will resist us vigorously.

The approach of Old Testament Levitical priests was to avoid putting themselves in a position of risk where they might defile themselves. They were very conscious of their calling and the need for holiness, which also means 'separation'.

Let me illustrate further. I have a 'father's anointing' and the Lord often calls me to be a substitute dad. Sometimes I need to give a young man or a young woman a father's hug, so I will always try to have someone with me as a protection, then I can safely allow God's father love to flow through me into that person. A fellow minister once said to me that he wasn't comfortable with what I was doing. I was willing to hear that, but I believe God wants to flow through me into others with the Father's love. I have to pray that if there is anything in me that needs people to look up to me that I will put it to death on the cross. If there is anything in me that needs a young woman or man to love me, I put it to death on the cross.

I made sure that I took all that the fellow minister said to the Lord and talked to Him about it. The trouble was that after that, I became afraid to hug anybody anymore or to offer myself. I made a promise to the people that I would be there for them, but then withdrew because I was frightened of being defiled. When I realized I had allowed the enemy to shut down what God wanted to do through me, in the end I would just go ahead and do it. My point is that, while being duly sensitive and careful, I am prepared to take risks for other people's sake so that death is at work in me and life is at work in them.

Old Testament holiness was separation. New Testament holiness is Jesus on a cross being defiled. Jesus is our righteousness and He has told us to love one another. If you are a burden bearer you are going to get slimed anyway! The answer is to take it to God in prayer and ask Him to give you a spiritual shower – a good washing down! Intercession originates in the heart of God and it is about God moving on man. The Holy Spirit sings over people and intercedes before the throne of God for them.

We have to be careful as musicians, worship leaders and artists to ask the question to whom and to what does our art connect people? God wants to draw hurt and sorrow to Himself and a burden bearer is one who naturally reaches out to draw the hurts of people. Musicians and artists are used by the Lord's Holy Spirit like an ink blotter soaking up the hurts of people. We must remember to release all of these to the Lord. He, living in us, is the true burden bearer, we only have the privilege of walking with Him in the *'fellowship of His sufferings'* (Philippians 3:10).

How do you know if you are a burden bearer? Generally speaking they have a unique personality type. It is made sensitive by God and they can sense spiritual vibrations in the atmosphere. They can often walk into a room and pick something up at once. They are very creative, very sensitive, and often have to battle with a lack of trust in their lives. The enemy tries to shut down this gift. As children many experience difficulty, some resent being born and cry a lot as children. Because they are so sensitive to other's feelings they sometimes close down their own, becoming over-serious and almost reclusive.

Often burden bearers need to learn how to play with the Father and learn how to have fun, and to get around people they feel approval from who can draw them out. In some families you would see the burden bearing child as being out of step with the rest of the family. They can be very dreamy people, may have bad memories, and people call them different. Sounds like musicians to me! As teenagers they can feel anger very easily and fall into depression. They have a deep need to be understood and often develop a critical attitude to others while wrestling with who they are. Because of their deep-seated needs they often enter too deeply into dependent relationships. As young people they can resent life because it just seems too heavy a burden.

Prophetic praise, worship and intercession are becoming more and more important as God works His wonderful restoration in the earth. As we stand before the Lord (as in Isaiah 48:9), He says He will delay his wrath for the sake of His praise and He will not give His glory to any other. This is the dangerous place we find ourselves as worship leaders, musicians and artists. We are here to offer our heart and music as intercession to God in every arena of the world.

If this is so, then how can we experience the redemption of this gift so that it becomes a powerful ministry tool? I offer you six keys:

1. If you have discerned that you are a burden bearer, bring the gift before the Lord daily or at the very least every time you minister or play. Pray, 'Lord, I do not want to bear these burdens in my flesh, I want to release them to you.'

2. Pray for discernment to know the difference between your own burdens and other people's burdens; pray for protection in any unhealed area in your life.

3. Learn to recognize burden bearing as a call to intercessory prayer and keep the communication open between you and God all the time. Keep short accounts and walk in a spirit of repentance all the time.

4. Drink in worship, the refreshment of the Lord. Make sure you have fresh oil any time you minister (Romans 12:1).

5.   Develop your life so that you have balance and freedom.
     Don't allow yourself to be locked in. A good definition of
     the word balance is 'the ability to embrace all valid
     extremes'. It is not a tightrope. Let excess energy out
     through exercise and be really honest with the Lord
     about what you are feeling. Always tell God about how
     you feel. He knows anyway. Develop close, prayerful
     friendships and find someone to whom you can be
     accountable, who loves you for yourself and who is not
     trying to change you. Bring your need for approval and
     your need for self-importance to death on the cross –
     crucify it mercilessly. Don't neglect to meet together
     with God's people and learn how to separate the func-
     tions of your soul and your spirit. Hebrews 4:11–12,

> *'For the word of God is living and powerful and sharper
> than any two-edged sword, piercing even to the division of
> soul and spirit, and of joints and marrow, and is a
> discerner of the thoughts and intents of the heart.'*

This is a key scripture for burden bearers. Ask the Lord
to help you to know what is of you and what is of your
flesh and what is of your spirit. You need to know the
difference.

6.   Finally, Philippians 3:1 says,

> *'Rejoice, delight yourselves in the Lord.'*

Just enjoy Him and His presence and cultivate an
awareness that He is always, always with you.

Selah ...

'What a blessedness when I came to the knowledge that I had
been looking in the wrong place, when I found that victory,
sanctification, deliverance, purity, holiness – all must be found
in Christ Jesus Himself, not in some formula. When I claimed
Jesus just for Himself, it became easy and the glory came to
my life.'   (Albert Benjamin Simpson; 1843–1919)

Chapter 14

Zeal for God's House

The Bible tells us that the generation of the righteous shall be blessed. Throughout the Old Testament the Lord is constantly referred to as the God of Abraham, Isaac and Jacob, and clearly thinks and acts generationally. His desire is for one generation to tell the next about His goodness and for there to be an on-going process of discipling and training as each generation births the next. Each successive generation has to realize what it has inherited from the former generation – good or bad – and decide how it will influence those who follow on. We must develop in each successive generation an uncontainable zeal for God's house – a desire to honor Him with our lives, worship and community.

Everything that God gives is in seed form. The principle of sowing and reaping is a law that God has established. He invests in you and as you plant the seed of your own life into the ground, you experience death and resurrection – just as a growing seed does. What you sow, you will eventually reap. The sacrifice will be taken and burned before the Lord, then resurrection comes, and then the harvest. We are meant to reproduce ourselves into the next generation. It is a principle of life. We should be investing into those with whom we fellowship, to teach them and release their gifts, talents and abilities, so they eventually become better than we are. Anyone who has children knows this. What a great blessing for some young people to be minister's children, from a strong household in a godly generational line with strong parents and grandparents, because the Bible says that the generation of the righteous shall be blessed.

Have you ever felt like you are fighting with something you can't see? Fighting so hard for so long for such a small breakthrough? I believe that not only must we continually remind ourselves that we are in a spiritual war, we must also be aware that the battle passes from generation to generation. Sometimes we struggle with issues in our lives, desperately trying to find a solution, only to discover that previous generations of the family struggled with exactly the same problems. In the same way, as believers who are living under God's blessing, future generations will be blessed because of us. They will benefit from our obedience to the Lord. God loved King David so much that He promised to bless his generational line, even to the point where Jesus the Messiah was born from David's line, even though David was a murderer and an adulterer.

We need to see the bigger picture here. As a generation of musicians and creative artists, we have been called by God to impact our generation – every creative person desires to bring forth the things they feel inside and have them recognized by their peers – but we have also been called to train and positively influence the following generations. We must discover the fullness of God's blessing and glory and teach those who follow how to find it and live in it too. This is an essential part of God's generational plan.

It is possible for us to receive from God revelation of His plan for our destiny, our future and our purpose, and not only for us but for our children and our children's children as well. God has a plan for you and for the generation you alone can influence. There was a purpose for your birth and for your being here. The actions you take during your lifetime can be a blessing or a curse to your following generations. Take every opportunity to sow good seed, so that your successors will reap a great harvest.

The family line

If you are anything like me then you may not come from a godly line. My father was an alcoholic who betrayed the family and did many things that would promote generational curses. Yet here I am as a Christian and a pastor with a wife, three children and three grandchildren. I don't want my children and their children to inherit any generational curse. I don't want my own life to be affected by what my ancestors did either.

One of the things I was able to do, even though I had not seen my father for 25 years, was to fly to Australia to be with him when I discovered he was dying. I arrived literally just before he died and managed to make my peace with him. I told him that I loved him and what Jesus meant to me. I forgave and released him and in so doing obeyed the Bible by honoring my father, even though he may not have always been worthy of honor, despite the fact that I loved him dearly. The Bible says *'honor your father and mother that your days may be long in the land'* (Deuteronomy 5:16). It doesn't say honor your father and mother if they are worthy of it. It just says you honor them anyway. My dad died the last evening I was in Australia. I believe God kept him alive until I arrived. I stood over his deathbed and prayed and released myself and my family from all generational curses inherited down the family line.

I believe my family was freed from generational curses as we applied the blood of Jesus Christ to all of those things. We pronounced forgiveness to all those who had sinned against us and against whom we had sinned and said 'Lord bless our family and the future generations. What the enemy meant for evil you meant for good.' If Jesus comes back tomorrow that is fine by me, but if He doesn't I would like my children and my children's children to be blessed and not bound by things they cannot see. Commit yourself today to thinking and building generationally.

How to release generational blessing

In our church's school we are raising up children to be leaders. We are taking them through studies in leadership and showing them what a great leader Jesus was. I would like to suggest to you several ways in which you can promote generational blessing. Apart from the basic principles of honoring your father and mother, loving each other and doing good to one another, these are positive steps that you can take:

1. Raise all the Elishas that God sends to you

Elisha was hungry to learn from his mentor Elijah. Every Elisha sent by God who is hungry to know what you do and how you do it, teach them, raise them up, encourage them and bless them. Help them to become better at what they do than you. Elijah did fourteen miracles and he invested himself into Elisha, who called him his father. Elisha is on record as having twenty-five miracles so there was a double blessing on the investment.

2. Act on all the dreams that God has put in your heart

If you have been given a dream to become a wonderful worship leader and you know that it is God who has put this on your heart, well, He is not a cruel God! If He has said it then He will do it.

My middle daughter Alison had a dream in her heart that was given by God. Eventually it was wonderfully fulfilled, but it took much time and effort to work out. She spent a long time trying to be a ballet dancer, but she is 5 foot 9 inches tall – a beautiful looking woman, but totally the wrong shape for a ballet dancer and her feet are not small enough. She spent a lot of my money and a lot of both our time determined to be a ballet dancer. When her teacher finally said she would never make it she decided to be a ballet teacher. So she spent more of my money and more of our time and in the end her teacher said to her, 'Alison I really don't think you are going to make it at all.'

She was quite distressed by this and came and said, 'Daddy you have to talk to me.' I said to her, 'OK, tell me what God has put in your heart. What is your dream and your vision?'

She said she thought she had been trying to get something that God didn't want for her. When I asked her what she really wanted to do it took her a long time to answer the question. She had to go away and pray about it and she had a struggle. Eventually she came to me and told me what she really wanted to do. She really wanted to become a school teacher. The trouble was, when she was about 11 years old, we discovered that she had dyslexia. She couldn't spell, had difficulty reading and writing and often came to me in tears. I looked at her and said 'Alison, if God has put a dream in your heart He is not a cruel God. He would not give you a dream like that and then not give you the ability to do it. I don't understand it, but if you are telling me that God has put a dream in your heart to be a school teacher then I am willing to stand with you and pray with you and believe with you that God will give you the ability to do what He has put in your heart.'

So together we fasted and prayed and talked to people and sought God. Every time I saw Alison I even said to her, 'Hello, you school teacher.' We thanked God for the school teacher that God had given us. At the same time as all this was going on my wife became pregnant again, but this time not with a baby! This time it was a vision to bring up children under the lordship of Christ in a Christian school. Three years later God miraculously allowed Alison to qualify as a teacher through a series of seeming coincidences where she met people who took her on board and trained her. Today she is one of the most anointed children's teachers I have ever met and she teaches at our own school.

In Alison's class there was one child of Muslim parents. This little girl would have fits and her mother would end up at the hospital with her every five weeks or so. She spent one term with Alison and God healed her and she did not go back to the hospital again. The anointing on my daughter is so strong. Basically it is because she dared to believe God in spite of circumstances and God anointed her life. She pioneered our school and at this time we have a primary school with almost 70 children in it. She started a senior section one year ago! The non-Christian mums and dads all know about this little girl who got healed. They recommend our school to their Muslim friends and they say 'Look what their God did for my little girl.' It is incredible. So always act on the dreams God has put in your heart. They are the purposes of God in you trying to burst out.

3. Teach children the value of Jesus Christ

Children tend to know the price of everything but not the value of things. Make sure that you build godly values and principles into their lives. Teach them not to be consumers but producers and to be fruitful. If you take the time to invest in them, they will take the time to invest in the next generation.

4. Promote the gospel

Use your time to the glory of God. When you have found out what you are meant to do, learn to be content in it. There are only two reasons for being discontented: either you have not found what you are supposed to be doing, or you are doing what you are supposed to but haven't made your mind up to enjoy it. You could waste your whole life looking for something else. If you are doing what you are supposed to, delight yourself in it and thank the Lord for it. Make sure you are happy doing it.

5. Develop your zeal for the Lord

I had a dream recently. I was in a large auditorium with new carpets, shiny flight cases and instruments lying around, a big grand piano in the corner, a lot of light rigging and a great sound system. I asked the drummer to help me to soundcheck the PA system. In my dream the drummer got hold of a snare drum in one hand and casually sat on the drum riser and began to bang the snare drum into the microphone. It wasn't enough so I asked him to put the whole kit up so we could sound check properly. The drummer said to me he could not be bothered as it was too much trouble. I found myself getting very angry at this point.

Over the other side at the wonderful grand piano was a young girl sitting playing the piano, and she was very flashily dressed. She was playing well but showing off with a very technical, fast piece of music, and playing it so loudly that it was obtrusive and I couldn't hear what others were saying. I turned round to talk to her and said 'Excuse me,' intending to ask her to stop for a moment. She did what all of you have done as musicians and pretended not to hear! She definitely heard me but pretended she hadn't. I repeated myself and she ignored me, so I went over to her and said 'I recognize that piece of music you are playing and I recognize that it takes a lot of skill to play it, but I don't appreciate your showing off your technique, and in any case, you need a lot more practice because you are not playing it right. Get off my stage and go and practice in the back where nobody can hear you.' She was not happy and went away in a bad mood.

I said to the drummer 'Listen, you are one of the finest Christian drummers in Europe and you can't be bothered to serve the Lord properly. If it is too much trouble for you to set up so that we can have a proper sound-check, then you can go home and let someone else do the job!' I was not happy and I felt this passion rising up in me because I knew that these people had selfish ambition in their hearts. They were not doing it for the Lord, they were doing it for themselves. They were more concerned about how wonderful they were and what other people thought of them than thinking about trying to serve the Lord in His house and trying to beautify the place.

Galatians chapter 5 says that selfish ambition is a work of the flesh. James 3:13 says that jealousy and envy are the brothers of selfish ambition and lead to disorder and every evil practice. I felt that the Lord was saying to me in the dream that there was a zeal that God wanted to put on musicians, that they would abandon selfish ambition and become consumed with a passion for God's house.

Psalm 69:9 speaking of Jesus says that, *'Zeal for your house has consumed me.'* This prophetic scripture alluded to the time when Jesus, full of zeal, would drive the money changers out of the temple (John 2:17). We need to have that sort of zeal for God's house.

Galatians 4:18 says it is good to be zealous for the Lord providing the purpose for your zeal is good. Be zealous always and not just when people are looking. Developing a secret history with God is very precious.

We must align our thinking with God's if we are to see the next generation come into the fullness of His blessing. God wants us to play our part, sow good seed, and release His blessing to others. Professional musicians have often talked of 'paying their dues' – in other words they say to the youngster trying to make his way, 'I'm not going to give you your big break until you've played your share of seedy nightclubs and lousy audiences – you've got to earn the right to succeed.' God does not work like that. He turns the world's logic on its head and says to Christian musicians and artists, 'Give all your secrets away! Help the next generation to find their way; help them to climb higher and reach further than you did. Release my blessing!'

Selah...

'May God Almighty bless you and make you fruitful and increase your numbers until you become a community of peoples. May he give you and your descendants the blessing given to Abraham, so that you may take possession of the land...' (Genesis 28:3–4)

Coda

Bringing it All Together

God's plan for every person is that they should reach their full potential in Him, that they should worship Him whole-heartedly and openly, in spirit and in truth. In order to do this we need to allow Him to have full control and access in our lives so that we can receive healing from Him that will enable us to be truly whole people. As we allow God to touch and shape our lives, we will become progressively fulfilled because our gifts will be released and we will begin to function just as God always intended us to.

As we begin to co-operate with God's plans and purposes, we will see a mighty outpouring of God's Spirit resulting in prophetic, evangelistic, warfare worship – Intercession that will shake the foundations of the kingdom of darkness and bring light to our cities. God is about the business of raising up an end-time army of Levites, and just as in the time of King David, creative worship will be on the frontline, herald-ing the victory of the Lord, the Mighty God of Israel.

Pray that church leaders everywhere will grasp hold of the importance of reconciling creative artists who have been disenfranchised, back to the Church; to work together to heal those broken relationships; to seek to understand the heart of the creative person, and with God's help, release them into fulfilling their God-given potential as their gifts find their true voice. I also pray that they will pursue this healing for themselves, becoming better leaders in the process.

The glory that man forfeited in the Garden of Eden when he traded the truth for a lie will be restored when we lay aside all our personal agendas and really listen to what God is saying to us. Francis Frangipane expresses this truth well in his book, *The Days of His Presence*:[1]

> 'The world will see the Lord Jesus Christ accompanying His Church in profound displays of glory. Great power from God shall seek out and rest upon those who are choosing now to humble themselves before Him. Without hype or self-promotion, the Presence of God shall again be revealed ... It is true that no one has seen the Father's glory, but God the Son has manifested Himself in glory numerous times in the past. In truth, the Bible was written by people who had seen the glory of God.'

God's plan was always that mankind should be covered in the love, the glory, and the presence of God. Since the fall, when our ancestor Adam lost that covering, mankind has constantly searched to find an adequate covering for his fear and shame. This he looks for in many things, including his own creativity, but he will never truly find rest until he finds his rest in God. **This** is the Lost Glory.

The days ahead

In the days ahead, God will call men and women to form whole communities of artists and musicians to pioneer a new Levitical order, according to Malachi 3:2–5 and 2 Chronicles 20. They will pursue not only artistic excellence and pioneer new things in creativity, but also spur one another on to reach new heights in creative thought and discipline – the kind of 'coloring outside the lines' creativity so loved by God. They will love God with their whole hearts and pursue His presence with all their might, being fully committed to wholeness and the true freedom that comes from the Spirit of God. These artists and musicians, intercessors and prophets will be prepared to drain every drop from their gifts in order to give the glory to the Giver Himself. They will reach up to heaven and take the Kingdom by force, filling up the airwaves and light-waves with the reflected glory of God. God will at last have a company of Levites who will be able, as in David's day, to bring the very presence of God into our towns and cities. They will refuse to break rank or fall away when attacked, because they are aggressively pursuing their sanctification. They will refuse to bow the knee to oppression and temptation in any form.

Just as the historical Renaissance drew together a new generation of artists with fresh ideas that impacted the world, I believe that there is a greater Renaissance to come, when God Himself will call artists together to fill the earth with beauty, and who are as gifted as the great musicians and artists of the past but totally filled with His Holy Spirit, possessing the balance of refined character along with exceptional gifting. What a statement to the nations that Jesus Christ is Lord, bringing glory to God the Father!

New centers of blessing

As God raises up new communities of artists, these groups will be like wells of blessing in the earth. The ones who will last will be wise enough to center themselves around ministries that can properly care for them and support them in their quest. These communities will be under the anointing of godly order and authority, because the leaders themselves will have the same priorities of dedication to wholeness and sanctification, and therefore become leaders who are much easier to follow! The Spirit of God will then be given His rightful place to move creatively and beautifully again, hovering over God's creation. Church will never be the same again, and God will get the glory!

Selah . . .

'Nearer and nearer draws the time, a time that shall surely be;
When the earth shall be filled with the glory of God,
As the waters cover the sea.'   (Traditional hymn)

'God will have the last word and it will be good.'
                              (Robert H. Schuller; 1926–)

By the grace of God, we prophesy to the 'dry bones' of the artistic community to come together in common purpose and vision – that the sinews and joints of good relationships may come together in communities under godly authority. As they begin to emerge, Holy Spirit would you breath life into them and cause them to receive healing, and be set free to worship God with their gifts under your anointing. As they give themselves to Your purposes, please use them as intercessory prayer warriors who will form the vanguard of the end-time army, called of God to usher in the healing of the nations as You inhabit their praises Lord. 'O God, that You would breathe on these slain and cause these bones to stand up and live and bear fruit, and the earth shall be filled with Your **Glory**.'

Note

[1] Frangipane, Francis. *The Days of His Presence*, New Wine Press, 1995, p. 17.

For further reference

I referred extensively to *A History of Western Music* by Donald Jay Grout whilst researching this book, published by J.M. Dent & Sons, London, 1960.

Kevin J. Conner, *The Tabernacle of David*, Portland, Oregon, City Bible Publishing, 1976.

Watchman Nee, *Spiritual Authority*, New York, Christian Fellowship Publishers, 1972.

Quotes for the *Selah*'s were taken from *Drapers Book of Quotations for the Christian World* by Edythe Draper. Wheaton, Illinois, Tyndale House Publishers, Inc.

If you have enjoyed this book and would like to help us to send a copy of it and many other titles to needy pastors in the **Third World**, please write for further information or send your gift to:

Sovereign World Trust
PO Box 777, Tonbridge
Kent TN11 0ZS
United Kingdom

or to the **'Sovereign World'** distributor in your country.